To Be a Girl To Be a Woman

Ruth Vaughn

To Be a Girl
To Be a
Woman

Fleming H. Revell Company
Old Tappan, New Jersey

Scripture quotations are from the King James Version of the Bible.
Scripture quotation from *The Living Bible,* copyright © 1971 by Tyndale House Publishers, Wheaton, IL. Used by permission.

Excerpt from "You've Got to Be Carefully Taught," Copyright © 1949 by Richard Rodgers and Oscar Hammerstein. Copyright Renewed, Williamson Music Co., owner of publication and allied rights throughout the Western Hemisphere and Japan.
International Copyright Secured
ALL RIGHTS RESERVED
Used by permission.

Excerpts from "A Different Sort of Liberation," by Carolyn Lewis © 1977 by The New York Times Company. Reprinted by permission.

Library of Congress Cataloging in Publication Data

Vaughn, Ruth.
  To be a girl, to be a woman.

  1. Femininity (Psychology)   2. Femininity (Philosophy)
3. Adolescent girls.   4. Marriage.   5. Women and
religion.   I. Title.
HQ1206.V3   1983   305.4′2   82–12263
ISBN 0–8007–1328–1

FOR BILL
Who made my dreams come true

Contents

Who Are You?

One

A Teenager's Prayer

God, here I am in a "chaotic state"
Seeking some way to do "something great" . . .
I want to be someone who contributes to make
A less violent world for everyone's sake . . .
But who can I go to and who can I trust,
Who'll show me the difference between love and lust?
I'm willing to listen, I'm willing to do
Whatever it takes to make this world "new" . . .
But in the confusion and the noise all around
Where can the answer to my question be found?
Dear God up in heaven, hear a teenager's plea—
Show me somewhere what You want me to be!

HELEN STEINER RICE

Who Are You?

What does it mean . . . *to be a girl?*

    Twelve . . . Emerging from childhood
                Impressionable as clay
                Easily bruised, like a flower,
                Combustible as dynamite
                Dreaming of being a woman . . .

    Fourteen . . . Winding up like a top to spin into maturity
                  Eating excitement like chocolate sundaes
                  Chomping curiosity like popcorn balls
                  Jumping up and down with desire for adventure
                  Dreaming of being a woman . . .

    Sixteen . . . Approaching the miracles of life that are still ahead
                  Untouched and unopened
                  Like Christmas as a child

                  Feeling the magic blowing ever-closer, hauntingly sweet,
                  Like Beethoven's Ninth

Believing the glory of all life *can* be

Unbolting doors; flinging out windows; spreading wide the
arms;
    Letting Life flood in *all* dimensions
    Of spirit, mind, and soul

Dreaming of being a woman . . .

Eighteen . . . Emerging from girlhood
        Bent on discovery
        Reaching for the overflowing cup
        Tiptoeing for the other side of the rainbow
        Learning to love self and others equally,
            as Christ commanded
        Thinking more; talking less

    Becoming a woman . . .

What does it mean . . . *to become a woman?*
    It means to be creative.
    Women were formed by God to be creative physically.
                        Creative emotionally.
                        Creative mentally.
                        Uniquely.

A man cannot create a new life inside his body.
A man cannot create an emotional atmosphere
    in the sensitive dimension of a woman.
A man cannot perceive things
    in the distinctive way the feminine mind operates.

Woman's point of view is diverse from man's
    One is not superior
    Each is singularly special.

You are becoming a woman . . .
    Perceiving, analyzing, feeling
        in ways the noncreative gender never can.

At times wrapped up
    in layers of confusion, frustration, bewilderment, fear

But deep inside, waiting
Waiting until you are ready

To leave girlhood and turn t
                             h
                             a
                             t corner *to be a woman.*

What will it be like *to be a woman?*
  Open to the sun
  On the face
  And the soul
  Whole
  Daring to reach
    For your Best Tomorrow . . .
    You . . . You . . . *You* . . .
    You are becoming a woman!

And it is the most wonderful feeling in the world!
  Rejoice in it.
    And give thanks.

God Knows
Who You Are

2

When I was a teenager, I would look in the mirror, sometimes by the hour, and wonder, *Who are you?*

My reflected brown eyes gazed earnestly back at me.

There was no answer.

The girl-in-the-looking-glass didn't know *who* I was. But God did.

I didn't know that then.

I can remember times, in the change from girl to woman, when I would throw myself across the bed sobbing, "I can't stand it!
                                                    I can't stand it!"

Over and over, I cried the words.

I had no idea *why* I was crying.

I had no idea *what* it was I couldn't "stand"!

I was reacting to changes, forces, complexities, contradictions in my life which I, as a youth, could not comprehend.

But God did. Even then.

But I didn't know.

As you and I ponder together on girl becoming woman, I want to tell you some things that are important. Had I known them, I would have been spared a lot of torment. Now that I have learned these lessons, I want to tell you, to help you bypass that pain.

This is what I want to tell you.

You are never alone.

God is with you.

Not only that . . .

God knows who you are.

Isn't that exciting?

You don't know inside your head yet.

The girl-in-the-mirror can't tell you.

But the almighty God knows who you are.

Because He created you.

In your personal creation, God endowed you with the talents, interests, aptitudes, and perceptions that you have. On purpose. Because, as Creator, He had a dream of who you would be as girl, as woman.

You are not a biological accident. No matter how many stories, jokes, or textbook explanations you've heard, the truth remains that *you* are not a biological accident. You were deliberately, specifically created by the Almighty God. For a purpose.

Uproot all falsely preconceived notions about your creation.

Uproot all vagueness you have had about God's concern with you.

Sit very still and let the awe flow through your entire being: God knows who you are because God created you.

When you fully understand that, you may ask Him to take over your life in a new way. You may ask Him to forgive sins and guide you always.

You see, God not only knows *who* you are because of His creation.

God also knows *why* you are. God understands how everything that has happened to you since you were born has made you the person you are.

God knows why you are.

Two Fathers

When I was in college, my writing class was asked to draw, in words, a portrait of an important person in our lives. My friend and I both chose our fathers as subjects. Read these two sketches carefully and they will help you understand what I mean when I talk about *why you are.*

About my parent, I wrote:

My father's face shows kindness as some men's show vice and greed. His voice is rich and deep, like a river stretching out into the ocean. And as a child, when I listened to him read the part in the New Testament about love, the house was full of music. It wasn't just his enunciation that was good; it was the spirit in him that seemed to kindle a flame in the fine words.

He is a big man with wide shoulders and strong arms. I was six years old before I knew that the Bible was speaking of God rather than my father when it referred to the "everlasting arms." I heard it often and I always snuggled inside because I knew exactly how those arms felt. Every night, he'd grab me to his heart, fling me in the air, pull me back to safety, brush his lips across my cheek and then "the everlasting arms" would carry me to bed!

In my father lives a splendid simplicity and an unshakable honesty. You can always find him over there in the Sermon on the Mount, doing unto others as he desires them to do unto him.

There is no sophistry about this man. There is a power of plain goodness and kindness which shows in him like a campfire on a dark night. It is as warm as a campfire, too.

Immediately, you have an understanding *why I am*—attitudes, responses, values, perceptions—because you can clearly see the influence this one person had on my life. The *who* of Ruth is based, much, on the *why* of Ruth. Much of that latter is seeded in my relationship with this giant in my life.

On the other hand, you gain the same understanding of my friend as she writes about her father:

He was as thin as a stick man. His clothes hung on him like a scarecrow's. Although he bought expensive clothes, they always sagged on his emaciated frame. His face was lined with the scars of broken commandments. His smile was mocking and when his face was serious, his lips formed a cruel line.

His eyes were the most frightening. They appraised me often as a hunter would look at his quarry. I've never been hunting or seen the look in a hunter's eyes, but I'm sure I'm correct in the analogy because I was, indeed, his quarry. He tripped me for the fun of seeing me fall. He would offer me a cookie to get me close enough to slap. And when he was angry, I was the release-valve of his emotions. The imprint of his fists still mark my body.

From those brief paragraphs, you immediately know some of the major *why* of my friend. And you could quickly contrast her personality with mine.

God created the *who* of each of us uniquely. But the seeds of potentiality in each of us could grow into beautiful flowers or vicious thistles. Our response to our world determines how we grow. This is the *why* of our lives.

We are examining here only one force in the lives of me and my friend. And yet you immediately understand some things about *why*.

It is easy for me to believe in a loving God. My friend disdains the entire notion as wishful thinking.

It is easy for me to be trusting and giving. It is impossible for her to be trusting and giving unless one is proven in many ways for a very long time. And even then, those characteristics are hard for her.

It is easy for me to laugh. It is difficult for her to find humor anywhere in anything.

God knows why I am. One of the forces in that *why* is my response to one person in my life.

God knows the why of my friend. One of the forces in that *why* is her response to one person in her life.

God knows why you are. He understands the impact that your father and other vital people have made on your life. God also understands all the events, experiences, emotions, and other forces that are at work in every moment of your life.

When you jumped high with success, God was with you and He understood the power of that joy in your development of self-esteem.

When you walked slowly in defeat, God was with you and He understood the force of that pain in your development of self-esteem.

That is why I say: God knows why you are. Even when you don't.

After my friend wrote the character sketch of her father, she called me on the phone and said, "After putting the elusive memory of my father [he died when she was eight] into words that are tangible graphic reality, I have already come to an understanding of some of my starkest terrors."

But she was in college before that understanding came. She had never been able to guess, even remotely, the role her father played in the *why* of herself before.

Her father was a successful outgoing businessman and was declared "Jaycee of the Year" a few months before he died. The charm he showed to people outside his home were the things written in his obituary, stated in his eulogy. His child strained to have the same image of the man that others held. It had not occurred to her until she was a young adult studying psychology in a writing class that her father was responsible for the *why* of some of her "starkest terrors."

She did not know in her growing years. But God had been with her in her home and He understood. Then.

He is with *you* now and, just as with me and my friend, He understands you wherever you are in life, whatever are your circumstances. God knows. He totally, unerringly, and compassionately understands.

He knows about the happinesses, the sorrows, the loves, the hates, the "being included" with others, the feelings of alienation, the laughter, the tears, the securities, the terrors. God knows how each of those things has affected you.

• God understands who you are. He created you. He knows all your potential, all your seedling greatness, all you can become.
Even when you don't.
Even when no one else does.

• God understands why you are. He has been with you in every moment of life's experiences since conception. He knows your responses, whether good or bad, and the extent of each influence.
Even when you don't.
Even when no one else does.

• And because God knows, He will always lovingly be with you. He will always warmly accept you. He will always freely forgive you. He will always tenderly guide your life toward dreams' fulfillment—if you let Him.

You are never alone.

God Loves Who You Are

3

I made a list when I was in high school of who I wanted to be. I still have it. The list reads:

> Work to become . . .
> Like Shary in clothes
> Like Sandy in charm
> Like Margaret in piano
> Like Edna Rhe in humor . . .

And on, the list reads.

I laugh at it now. But I was dead serious then.

I wanted to be *like* Shary, Sandy, Margaret, and Edna Rhe. I wanted to be like these girls I admired because I didn't have the faintest idea who Ruth was!

Have you ever done that?

If you haven't actually written out the list on paper, you probably have made it in your head. Because, at this point in life, a girl so desperately wants to know the answer to: *Who am I?*

And you may have fallen into the same kind of trap I did.

Instead of spending my energies learning my true identity from God, I made lists and determinedly "worked toward being *like*" other people. And the price I paid for that dumb error was inferiority, frustration, and pain. For years.

I can now look at my friend Sandy and appreciate both the uniqueness of her charm and of mine. I never succeeded in emulating Sandy's charm. I have never, for a moment, been able to truly be *like* Sandy.

Sandy is a soft-spoken, low-key personality who is beautiful. I am a creative extremist with exuberance and idealism which send me soaring aloft on all kinds of impossible dreams and plans. But after years of self-hatred because I was not serene like Sandy, I now know that the bubbly joyful dreamer is also beautiful.

It was a glorious day for me when I discovered the word *unique.* I began to understand that I was specifically, distinctively different from Sandy, Shary, Margaret, and Edna Rhe. And that was all right.

All right . . . because I was Ruth.

Unique. One-of-a-kind.

I began to understand that I would never, try as I might, have charm *like* Sandy. I would never wear clothes with style *like* Shary. I would never play the piano *like* Margaret. I would never have a flashing humor *like* Edna Rhe.

I would have the charm of Ruth. I would wear clothes with the flair of Ruth. I would play the piano with the ability and expressiveness of Ruth. I would glow with the humor of Ruth. And all of those, combined with other elements, were the profile of a unique person who was as valuable as any other.

This is vital for you to understand.

There is no superiority among persons. There is no inferiority.

Just as Sandy is unique in her charm, so am I.

Just as Sandy is a valuable person because of her soft gentleness, so am I valuable because of my exuberant dynamism.

One is no greater than the other.

Both are unique.

Both are of inestimable value.

I watched an interview on television the other day with the world-famous pianist, Artur Rubinstein. As a routine question, he was asked his reaction when he is called "the greatest pianist in the world."

Artur Rubinstein replied, "I become angry. There is no such thing as 'best.' Each person is unique. There is no best. There is only *difference.*"

I was delighted with Rubinstein's conviction. Proclaimed almost unanimously by world critics as the best, he merely argued that he was different! He asserted that many young pianists played technically better piano, but they didn't possess his spirit of music. This is what made him different, he said.

Ah! what glorious knowledge!

Stop for a while and consider this: Although you meet other people with varying skills, none will ever, ever, be better than you! They will be different! *And the two are not to be compared.*

Whatever you do, however you do it, you are as valuable as anyone else on earth. Work on that concept until you believe it.

Recently, the evening news featured a man who had given a huge art collection to a museum. It contained Picassos, Van Goghs, and other world-famous paintings. After a tour of the museum displaying the pieces was made via television camera, the curator said, "Did you keep any art pieces for yourself?"

The man smiled and said, "I kept the ones most meaningful to me."

The curator asked, "Could you tell us, then, the artist whose work brings you the greatest joy?"

The curator's bland smile turned to astonishment when the man said, "Yes. Valerie Davis. She's my daughter. Her works will never hang in a museum, but in my library they have always been the paintings most wonderful to me. Her colors, her energy, her joy all burst forth from the canvas. Those are the ones that make me happy."

The art collector's explanation makes this fact clear: There is no inferiority. There is no superiority.

More people will see and gain pleasure from the works of Van Gogh and Picasso. But numbers are unimportant. Valerie Davis's paintings made her father's heart sing. The expression of her talent was of equal value to the Van Gogh that made the curator's heart sing. They are different.

I often ponder on the impact of speech. Golda Meir used rhetoric to lead her country, Israel. Margaret Thatcher used it to become the first woman prime minister of England. My mother used it to mold the lives of her children. From infancy on, she had "special times" set aside for talking with us, sharing Bible stories and spiritual truths. All the time she was sweeping, cooking, and washing dishes, she was also speaking to us her philosophies of life.

Today, one of her sons is a minister; one is president of a Bible college; one is a colonel in the United States Army; her daughter is a professional writer. Could you really call Golda Meir or Margaret Thatcher *best* in setting forth their ideas? They influenced larger numbers of people. Economies and states and armies rested on their decisions. But was their impact of greater *value* than the mother who gave her finest speaking skills to four children?

There are larger and smaller audiences.
There is no superiority or inferiority between people.
There is only difference.

> Who are you?
> God knows and loves who you are.
> Why?
> Because *you* are special.
> Never-before-on-earth.
> Never-to-be-again.
> One-of-a-kind.
> Unique.
> Of inestimable value.

When you believe in that answer, you will never again strain to be *like* anybody. No matter how charming, winsome, delightful, talented, and beautiful another may be, you will be able to release her to be herself. You will be able to rejoice in all she is, for you will know that there is no competition, no superiority or inferiority between you.

- *You* are unique!
- *You* are one-of-a-kind!
- *You* are special!
- God knows and loves who you are.

And so will the people of your world because they will come to know, if they don't already, that no one can ever be like you.

God Loves
Who You Are—Now

4

When I came to believe that God did know that I was "different" from everybody else on earth, it was one of the most glorious moments of my life. I cartwheeled for months in the knowledge that God knew who I was and He loved who I was even though I would never be quiet like Sandy, stylish like Shary, or laugh like Edna Rhe.

He loved me because I was . . . one-of-a-kind Ruth!

I revelled in the knowledge.

I gloried in the healing it brought to deep spirit-wounds.

But I had still missed one important truth.

God knew who I was.

God loved who I was.

But I didn't know that He loved who I was. *Then.*

My problem was that I got hung up on the point that God loved me for who I would become, the finished dream. I could see the unique potential for the future, but that fulfillment was several years away. I was, at that moment, still filled with as many flaws as a flat tire.

The girl waiting to grow into the woman was filled with foibles. So I did not claim God's love for me then . . . and I was wrong.

This error caused me severe pain. And I now know it was completely needless.

When God created the uniquely special you—as child, girl, woman—He created you to enjoy your one-of-a-kind characteristics in each of those developmental stages.

God knows there will never be a woman like you when your potential is transformed into living reality.

But He also knows there has never been and never shall be a girl like you are. *Now.*

And He knows you . . . loves you . . . rejoices in you . . . just as you are. *Now.*

No changes asked.

No wistfulness about perfection.

No demands for future maturity.

I had three older brothers. That was supposed to be the family. But, with great shock, my parents discovered, at age fifty-three (my father) and forty-four (my mother), there was to be another one!

My brothers became dignified adults while I was still small. I remember that I was asked to be a flower girl in a wedding. I wore a long pink dress, and my hair was piled in curls.

At age five, I got through the wedding formality but as soon as we arrived at the reception (held out-of-doors), I ran, with relief and jubilance, to the great swing in the yard and began pumping out all my pent-up energies. When one of my brothers saw me, he was filled with consternation and came to reprimand me for my childish behavior.

Always deeply sensitive, always yearning to please, I was filled with self-hatred because I had embarrassed my family. It had not occurred to me that one did not swing whenever the opportunity afforded itself. I truly had not known what dreadful crime I was committing.

That night my father heard me sobbing in my bed. He came in and sat beside me, turning me toward him, brushing the curls off my hot sweaty cheeks. And when I confessed my shame, he laughed with love bounding all through the room. He grabbed me to him and said, "Honey, there are a lot of things your brother doesn't know yet. So let me tell you a secret. *Five-year-old girls are created for swinging.* I watched you flying high in your long pink dress and thought you were beautiful."

Incredulous, tears still streaming, I pulled back to study his face. "Are you sure?" I hiccoughed.

"I'm a very wise man," he grinned, "and I'm very, very sure."

He wiped my tears and lay me back on my pillow. "The time will come when you will stand in starched sedateness when you wear a pink formal.

I know that. And I will be proud of you because you will be becoming the lovely woman God meant you to be. But when you are five, you swing and jump and dance; you climb trees, hang from the roof beams, and walk on stilts. And I am proud of you. For you are the lively, energetic little girl that makes our house ring with joy."

I remember this incident so vividly because of the pain, the humiliation, the self-hatred caused by my brother's reprimand. I remember the shriveling of my heart, the welling up of despair that I would ever be able to please, the certainty that I could never be of value.

I felt it all during the rest of the reception, all the way home, all the time I was getting dressed for bed. I hadn't even taken time to pray beside my bed because the tears were so close. I knew that when they came, it would be the release of a flood. And then, in the midst of all that suffering, my father assured me that he knew I would, one day, be a lovely, sedate woman. And he would be proud. But, at the moment, I was a *"Five-year-old girl . . . created for swinging!"* And he had watched me fly through the air, long pink dress and all, and rejoiced. *Now.*

He sat with me that night, and I gained my first clue of love that accepts, enfolds, and rejoices in . . . whoever I am at whatever moment of life I happen to be.

No changes asked by my father.

No wistfulness about perfection.

No demands for future maturity. Even in a long pink dress.

He loved me. *Now.*

Jesus said God is like the earthly father who loves, accepts, welcomes his child. Always. It is true.

If you will fully believe this, you can walk through life with all of its complexities with a peace that passes all understanding. Why?

God knows who you are . . . You will never be misunderstood.

God loves who you are . . . You will never be unacceptable.

Now . . . You will never, not even for a moment, walk alone.

Who Will You Become?

Two

This Is
All I Ask

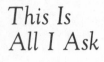

Lord, show me the way
I can somehow repay
The blessings *You've* given to me . . .
Lord, teach me to do
What *You* most want me to
And to be what *You* want me to be . . .
I'm unworthy I know
But I do love *You* so—
I beg *You* to answer my plea . . .
I've not got much to give
But as long as I live
May I give it completely to *Thee!*

HELEN STEINER RICE

Who Will You Become?

I

My mother was a schoolteacher when she married my preacher-father. She had been for several years.

Today, we would call her a "career woman." In that era, she was considered an "old maid." But she cared little. She had an ongoing adventure with life. She loved people; she loved sharing; she was beautiful, intelligent, and had an insatiable joy for living.

On the wall of my room, I had a large oval-shaped photograph of her as a young woman. Through all my growing years, I studied it. I knew I was much like her physically. We were both tiny of stature, slight of frame, with dark hair and eyes.

But as I looked at the picture, I could see, burning in her eyes, a flame, like a glowing candle, that made her radiate love, courage, strength, gentleness, kindness. Any stranger could see it, I believe, but I, her child, considered it carefully. Because I knew it was everlasting. I had grown in its warm brightness every moment of my life.

Sometimes I would take the photograph off the wall and hold it beside my face as I looked in the mirror. *Who will I become?* my heart questioned? *Will I be like my mother?*

My heart plummeted to my toes.

Of course, I would not be *like* my mother. To me, she was perfection. I could never, ever, be like her.

So if not her, who then?

I had no idea. And with a sigh, I would hang the old-fashioned oval frame back on the wall and wonder disconsolately how one ever found the way from girlhood to womanhood.

And then one day I was given a clue.

It was suggested that a good method of self-discovery was to take a notebook in hand and write out, specifically, personal desires, personal goals, personal dreams. No one else would ever see it. I could, thus, privately and honestly explore who Ruth *might* become.

The challenge was: Consider very honestly what is true for *you*. Not for Mother, as much as I admired her. Not for the sedate lady my brother seemed to want me to be. I was asked to write, in the light of God-given perception, the *who* of Ruth.

It was the best method of answering *Who am I to become?* that I have found. It worked for me. It has worked for my sons. It has worked for my students.

Let me tell you about its use in the life of a girl named Janet.

When I was a college professor of speech and creative writing, Janet rushed on campus as a freshman, telling us all that she had been "called of God" to be a college teacher in the communication area. She believed that with full heart as she faced her initial semester.

Those first weeks, she had nothing but academic problems. Educational techniques bored her; the rules of creative writing made her restless; public speaking skills were incompatible with her shy, inarticulate personality.

After failing an important exam, she came to my office in tears. She hated herself and felt that her academic inadequacy was a spiritual problem.

As we talked, we began exploring what things were *true* to Janet. Her eyes sparkled when she talked about electronics, radio transmitters, and all kinds of things about which I knew nothing.

When we discussed public speaking, challenging students to learn, giving of oneself in a classroom, her eyes took on a hunted, cowed look.

I challenged Janet to try the method I had used of sifting through all the things others had dreamed for her and discover for herself what was true to her God-created nature.

She agreed to try.

When she returned to my office, the defeated, self-despising look was gone. There was a spring in her step as she bounded in and placed a list on my desk. I was not surprised that, on it, I found no trace of the words *college teacher.*

That, she informed me in the new wonder of self-discovery, had come from her mother who had been a college speech teacher prior to her marriage. She wanted to relive that professional joy through her child, and Janet had, unconsciously, agreed.

But when Janet took the time to look deeply, with God, at what was true to the uniqueness of herself, she found that she loved the technical side of radio more than anything. That was the kind of knowledge she could easily learn because it was fascinating to her. There, she could excel because that was true to Janet's God-created dream—not her mother's.

It was a difficult transition.

She had to be honest with herself, with her mother, and with her friends to whom she had proclaimed so loudly the other dream. She had to turn from one road onto another. It was not easy. Change never is.

But today, Janet is using her special expertise in technology with and for missionaries. She makes possible communication in areas where it had never been before. She is serving her church in an invaluable way; she, the one-of-a-kind Janet, experiences complete personal fulfillment.

Try this method of self-exploration. Get yourself a notebook and pen. Or, if it is easier, just write in the margins of this book. But try, along with God, to honestly identify those characteristics, traits, aspirations, dreams, goals that are true to you.

Make the list as long as you can. Dream as wide and high as possible. No one is going to see this but you and God. So let go and write with abandon.

When you have finished, go back over each item and consider it carefully with God. Is this really true to you or is this item on your list because of a desire to please someone you love and admire? It is vital, as you look at your list of potentials, that you scrutinize each of them in light of whose idea it is.

If it is not your own, cross it off.

That can often shrink a list. But that's good. For it is important self-knowledge. You cannot grow into the woman God created you to be when you are dreaming of being someone else!

So carefully consider each ideal on your list.

If it isn't there because *you* dream it, if it isn't there because of a God-created love for it deep within *you,* cross it off. Be true to you as you explore, with God, the possibilities of who you will become!

Who Should You Become?

2

Who will you become? The answer is based on the choices that you make and, as we saw in the example of Janet, it is possible to make wrong decisions that can affect all of your life.

Who should you become? This is the query that can lead to right decisions. The answer to that question can only come through self-knowledge of what is true to the God-created uniqueness of you.

Let me tell you about my student, Valerie.

In her first semester of college, Valerie struggled with the course I taught on the Fundamentals of Public Speaking. It was dreadful for her.

She was always on the verge of tears when she stood in front of the class. One day, the dam broke in the midst of a speech and she began to cry. Embarrassed beyond help, she rushed from the room.

I dismissed the other students and ran after her. I brought her, still sobbing, to my office.

There, behind closed doors with a lot of Kleenex available, she told me all about her beautiful sister who won State in debate, starred in the high school production of *Carousel,* won a college scholarship in speech, and was now a food-show hostess on local television.

When she finished with the story of her sister's incredible achievements, I asked, "But Valerie, what about you?"

She looked at me in surprise.

"What about me?"

"Your sister's talents are lovely," I told her. "But that has no real bearing on what *is* for you!"

I could see the pain in her eyes. I was her speech professor. Was I going to close the door on her being like her sister?

"Oh, I'll get over this baby stuff," she promised tensely. "I guarantee I will never cry again. I can do that because I will try so hard. . . ."

"Why do you have to try so hard?" I asked.

The tears came again.

"Because speaking doesn't come easily to me as it does to my sister. She adores it. I am terrified." Her head went into her arms; her shoulders heaved. "Oh!" she shuddered, "Oh, how I wish I never had to give a speech again!"

When the storm of weeping finally passed, we talked about what was true to the uniqueness of self. She agreed to open herself to the Creator-God and seek to discover God's dream for the one-of-a-kind Valerie.

It was hideously painful. It meant giving up the question she had answered long ago—Who *will* I be?—and changing it to the query, Who *should* I be?

Valerie was so bound up in wanting to be like her sister that it took much time, many tears, and hours of thought readjustment to be able to perceive that it was all right for her to have no interest in speech. It was all right for her to be unlike her sister. And when she reached that plateau, she was able to open herself to "knowing" God's dream for the special Valerie.

She had grown up on a rich Kansas farm. She found all aspects of it exciting and beloved. To her, my, and everyone's amazement (except her knowing father), she discovered, alone with God and a notebook for self-exploring, that what would truly bring her the greatest satisfaction was farming. With that self-knowledge, she gained the poise to get through the hated-but-required speech class. Then she changed her major to agriculture.

Now with a glowing tan, muscular as Olga Korbut, this one-hundred-ten-pound young lady will soon graduate from college. She regularly runs up a long-distance telephone bill apprising me of her plans for improving the yield on her father's farm as soon as she can be there full-time. I listen to her discussion of the alien (to me!) subject of agriculture with complete delight. Her enthusiasm is vibrant proof to us both that she knows God's special dream for Valerie.

How strained and unexciting would be her life were she now graduating from college as a speech major, simply because she found that to be a beautiful quality, characteristic, career for her sister!

Planting crops, working in fields, figuring yields-per-acre are true to Valerie. That, she now finds, is a beautiful quality, characteristic, career for herself.

Not superior to her sister. Not inferior.

Equal. Different. Valuable.

Now she knows the answer to that vital question: Who should I become?

That is what I am now asking of you.

Look at your personal list.

Run each item through the filter:

Is it really true to me

or

Is it something I admire in someone else?

Be thoroughly honest. Don't get caught in the trap as Valerie did.

God made you unique, one-of-a-kind. Don't settle for being like someone else, no matter how admirable she may be in her own uniqueness.

Carefully consider the characteristics, attributes, careers you have written. Cross off each item unless you and God both know it is a part of His special dream for you.

Reach for your special star and you will find the answer. Who should you become? You should become the unique fulfillment of God's creation of you.

Could You Take the Dare?

3

In the musical, *The Man of La Mancha,* there is the song that challenges each listener to "dream the impossible dream." It is a stirring lyric with a rousing musical beat that flourishes into the dare to "reach the unreachable star."

In considering the query *Who should I become?* you must never limit God. Remember you are in relationship with the Creator of such incredible achievements as the Grand Canyon, the Milky Way, and the Rocky Mountains. Be open, in this moment, to allow Him to point you to glories you may have felt were beyond your reach.

God dreamed a beautiful dream when He created you. And if you find a great yearning for something that your mind tells you is unattainable for any reason, take time to consider this possibility prayerfully in His Presence. Don't be afraid to reach for the "unreachable star" as you pray. God may have placed that yearning there in the uniqueness of His plan for you. And if that be true, He will open doors that will astound you. He will stretch you so that you will be able to fulfill every dimension of each God-planted dream.

You are not living your life alone. You are allowing the Sovereign God to live His abundant life in you. His dreams are grand and wide in His creation. Be open to allow Him to dream His finest dreams in you now, as He did when He made you.

Let me tell you about a girl who faced this challenge. Her heart's deepest longing was logically impossible. But she discovered that, with God, all things are possible.

Her name is Caroline. I received this letter a few years ago, and it is one of my most cherished possessions. As you read it, you will understand why.

Dear Ruth,

I walked across the platform tonight and received the Ed.D. in Music Education. After an exuberant celebration with my friends, I came to my apartment, took a hot bath, put on old pajamas, and sat down to reflect on the evening's activities. The diploma in my hands, I gazed at it with incredulity and wondered how it ever happened to bear my name.

My mind raced back to that awkward fourteen-year-old girl in a small town who had no options in life. I had no living father; my mother was a waitress; it was assumed I would be also. My love of music was simply that: a love of music. It would have no other bearing on my life.

And then there was that church basketball game when you came into the stands to sit with me. I, an unchurched girl, was awed that the minister's wife would come over to talk to me. But somehow it was true. I tried to carry on the conversation while studying you in bewilderment at your interest.

And then it happened.

I shall never forget the shock that went through me when you asked, "What are your life-dreams?"

You *assumed* that I *had* life-dreams that might not be obvious at first glance. I realized, then, you must not know who I was. I told you my family background. I told you my mother was a waitress. You didn't seem to make the connection. You told me that you did know my mother. You said she had a "wonderful way with people" in the restaurant. She was cheerful, helpful, and seemed happy in her work. But, what were *my* life-dreams, you persisted. And, to my total amazement, I blurted out, "I want to play the piano."

I looked at the Ed.D. diploma tonight and realized that it all began in that first confession to you that I wanted music to be a vital part of my life. *It was impossible,* of course. I'm sure you knew that. But you never let me know. And because you believed, so I came to believe.

I worked harder at my piano lessons; I entered and won contests; I tried out and was named accompanist for the high school choir; I ultimately won a piano scholarship to college. Gradually, God's beautiful life-plan unfolded and, astonishingly, it fulfilled that *true* heart-dream I had held all of my life.

But I would never . . . there is no question of this . . . I would never have gone beyond the city limits of that small town had I not had that moment of honesty with you at a church basketball game. In the flush of that self-knowledge, and enforced by your unswerving faith and encouragement, I proceeded to believe that my heart-dream might be significantly different than what seemed obvious for me in my life situation.

It *was* impossible.

No one in my family, on either side, had ever gone to college. Most people in our town were born there, lived all their lives there, and never went beyond. I had *no* precedent in my life to make me believe that I could be any different. Not until you.

Tonight that impossibility is reality.

That unique life-dream of mine, in God's great plan, came true. Because I was challenged to believe that what was *true* to me was God's dream for me.

Caroline's letter is, for me, a beautiful picture of a girl who answered the question, Who should I be? Although it seemed "an unreachable star," she dared to believe in her God-created uniqueness enough to reach for it. And, after years of an amazing series of God-miracles, she sat one night and penned me a letter, pausing now and then, I'm sure, to hold that star in her hands: a doctoral diploma in music.

But Caroline had to find "the star" as true to the one-of-a-kind Caroline before she could touch it. And that discovery came in the moment of truth she describes when she was fourteen. Had that perception never come to her, she firmly says that she would never have known the joyful fulfillment that now permeates her life.

This moment, as you sit with pad before you or as you scribble in this book's margins, you are, in a sense, in the most important period of your life. For you are facing choices that will mold all of your future. And those choices will be made in light of your understanding of your God-created true identity for the special *you.*

Is there some wonderful dream you never whisper out loud to anyone? God may have placed it there. It could be just for you! So if you find it, reach for it.

Reach, as did Caroline. You may, one day in the future, hold your "unreachable star."

Could You Make the Choice?

4

When I was in high school and college, many of my teachers and friends gave me lengthy lectures on the parable of the talents written in the New Testament. They stressed that I must be "found faithful" in giving all the necessary time and energy involved in perfecting my talents for God's use.

It was a good lecture.

But they left something out.

They never told me that one must be realistic about a limited amount of time and energy available. One must make choices, set up priorities, hierarchies of values. One must, with God, determine what talents, interests, aptitudes are "minors" and which is the "major."

If you have been scribbling on a pad or in the margins of this book, look at your list and understand that many of those things will be minors. Only a few majors. Perhaps only one.

It is not sensible to set out to "do your best" in many areas. It simply is not possible in twenty-four-hour days; seven-day weeks with no "wonder-woman" energies at your command.

Many counselors, ministers, teachers, even parents don't face that.

They set up idealistic goals for you and fill you with guilt when you do not reach them.

Let me tell you how a young woman I know met this dilemma.

When I began teaching freshman creative writing classes at college, I challenged each student to the kind of exploration that you and I have been talking about.

In one class was a girl named Janna. And after she had been working with her pad and pencil for a time, as you may have, she made an appointment to see me.

When she came to my office, she told me that she had gone out into a rural area, climbed a fence to sit under a tree, and opened herself to God with pencil and paper. As predicted, she had quickly, glibly written down her preset life-dreams. But in scrutinizing them carefully, with only God present, she became less sure.

In my office, she leaned back and took a deep breath.

She was bracing herself for the shock of her revelation to me.

"I discovered," she said, "that although I enjoy writing very much it isn't what I want to spend my life doing!"

She stopped to see if I could take the blow. Seeing that my reaction was minimal, she continued.

"Well, that makes me feel guilty! When I have won contests, showed off my first publications in the high school paper, written for the church bulletin, my family and friends impressed on me the obligation that I have to use this talent for God."

She leaned forward, straining in her earnestness.

"I want to do that! I truly do. But now that I begin to see what is involved in professional writing, I know this is not honestly my desire. Oh! I want to write," she hastened to assure me (she was still uncertain she was not uttering heresy) "it's just that, well, I know now that what I want most is to be with people. And writers aren't . . . I mean . . . there is so much solitary work in writing. I want to be with people."

Janna had discovered that although it was true that she wanted to write and God had given her an ability to write, it was only an interest—a *minor* in her life.

Her passion, her *major,* she had discovered was that she wanted to be with people! She now knew where to devote her best efforts to excel. That relieved her of the strain of giving "best efforts" to other interests and aptitudes. She would develop them, utilize them as there was time, energy, and opportunity.

Janna took an oral communication degree in college, a graduate degree in Christian education, and now finds fulfillment as minister of youth to a group of teens who make certain that she is, constantly, with people. That is her major!

She still writes. It's a happy, fulfilling minor.

She faithfully keeps her daily journal which gives her heart-release. She writes delightfully detailed letters which allow her family and friends to vicariously adventure with her. She writes prolific poetry which she sends to "her" teens on all birthdays, congratulation times, and "anytime" she feels one needed.

Yes, Janna uses the talent of writing, but in the dimension of self-expression—as a minor—not as the major life-dream.

If the ideas of "majors" and "minors" are new to you, you may look at the notes you have made on a pad or in the book margins and find the list shorter than you think it might be. Janna's list was lengthy, bulging with interests and dreams. You may have only written a couple of things and you may wonder why.

Perhaps it is because this is a new idea to you. Perhaps you have been content to move along smoothly with the status quo, assuming your future would be similar to others you know.

If you are interested, if you think your list of goals might be longer, set out on a search for what is available to you in this wide world.

Look at people about you—their careers, their hobbies. Watch television shows, especially those documentaries on PBS that will, often, take you on tours of fascinating places and show you careers that you may have never heard of, much less seen firsthand. Your local library has books dealing with careers, hobbies, interests, challenging ideas for your consideration. If you live in a large city, many schools and businesses have "career days" annually where youths are invited to explore possibilities for their life's work. The yellow pages can even give you a quick overview of a huge fascinating world where you can find the exact challenge most fulfilling for *you.*

It is easier to remain with what is familiar. It is easier to accept the precedent set for you by your family and peers. But I challenge you to go beyond the easy. Explore how gigantic and challenging and teeming with adventure is God's wonderful world.

After all that exploring, you may come back to exactly the first thing you wrote down. But if so, you will know, with greater certainty, that this truly is your heart-dream above all others.

I receive many complaining letters from women who whine that they gave up glorious careers to marry disappointing husbands . . . or take jobs in family businesses . . . or because they didn't know "women did anything else!" You will never become one of those unhappy women who sit about lunch tables with stories of "what might have been" if you thoroughly, carefully search all that is available for your future before you make your choice.

Whatever field interests you, you may shoot for the top spot: being a doctor in a children's hospital, being the editor of a newspaper, being the lawyer pleading her case in court. You may find that such heavy-responsibility, limelight positions hold no fascination for you. But you may find you would enjoy working as a therapist in a children's hospital, being a reporter on a newspaper staff, or being a law clerk who researches the lawyer's case.

My school chum Andrea chose the latter goal. It means hours of working alone, going through hundreds of dusty old books to find court precedents and other needed information for building a lawyer's court case. Andrea shares the excitement of her work with me, and I thoroughly enjoy it, for I find personal challenge in research.

Andrea received her training to be a legal secretary in public high school courses. Upon graduation, she gained a job in a legal firm. After she had proven herself, the firm paid for her training as a legal clerk.

So, when you peruse potential areas of challenge for your future, don't let the thought of finance deter you. There will always be a way—if it is the true God-given dream for you. I have seen it proven in the lives of hundreds of determined people. When you know your true God-dream, He will enable you to make it become reality—if you work with Him and are open to His leadings.

When you know, work "faithfully," as my teachers and friends used to urge me, to "give your very best" to the major of your life. But understand, as they did not help me understand, that there are only a few *majors,* maybe only one, in anyone's life. All of those other interests and aptitudes that are true to you are *minors,* grace notes, to be developed and used as possible. But you are under no pressure to "give your best" in these areas.

This is vital self-knowledge that will allow you to live your life to optimal fulfillment with none of the pressures for perfection in all areas.

Understand *your* majors.
Know *your* minors.
With God, make your choice and be at peace.
For all of your life.

Could You Believe in Your Choice?

5

When you make your choice of the majors and minors in your life, there will be people who will disagree. Some may be vehement in stating their disapproval to you.

When you are still finding God's leadings, you may want to consider others' words carefully and pray about them deeply. But once you know—deep inside where there is no question—the "unreachable star" that is true to the God-created you, do not be deterred by others' opinions.

In the last chapter, we talked about Janna who, in my creative writing class, discovered that although writing was nice, she didn't want to spend her life with words. She wanted to be with people. And yet, at the moment of her first joy of admission to me, she said that the happiness was a bit tainted because she felt guilt. Those who knew of her writing ability made her feel a sense of pressure to become a published writer.

Another student, Kyndi, told me that she starred as "Marian, the librarian," in her high school production of *The Music Man.* After curtain call, Kyndi was deluged with people telling her that they were "counting the days" until they saw her starring on television.

Kyndi said, "My whole being cringed. This was fun, sure! For high school. But I didn't want to do it all my life. I wanted to be a wife and mother. These people made me feel guilty that my goal wasn't professional acting."

This can happen to you.

As you discover, with God, more about the uniqueness of you, your life-direction may do a complete turn. Your previously held values may change. What you once considered a major, you might, now, believe to be a God-intended minor.

And people may misunderstand. They may be disappointed.

They may hand you a huge basket of guilt . . . and you're in for a lot of frustration if you accept it. Even though they put that basket on your doorstep, you can choose to walk away from it.

No one can force you to feel guilty unless you allow them.

When you are certain you and God have understood-values on the various facets of your life, you are no longer responsible for other people's opinions. When these people truly know you and care deeply about you, you may want to recheck your list with God to be sure your choices of majors and minors are correct. But when you and God are at peace, when you and He have a mutually pleasing agreement on this matter of majors and minors, you must choose to walk through life free of any guilt people on the outside may try to impose.

This was one of my most severe torture-points. I have already mentioned that high school and college teachers and friends spent hours with me trying to impress on me the responsibility of my talents and their potential use for God. I was extremely conscientious. I wanted to please God with my whole being. I wanted to please other people.

And so, not understanding then about majors and minors, I picked up my list of interests and aptitudes and set out grimly to be "the best possible" in each area. I kept myself on a rigid schedule, working from early till late.

During my freshman year in college, I overcommitted myself. I was in so many activities I hardly had time to eat or sleep. Surely I had no time for fun and relaxation.

One of the pressures I had accepted was playing the lead role in a college play. One night during rehearsal, I fainted center stage! Now how's that for good drama?

At the time, I was dating a young man with an overabundance of common sense. (He is now my husband which proves that I did have *some* common sense, too.) After the college nurse was rushed to the stage and I was properly revived, my both-feet-on-the-ground boyfriend said he would escort me to the dormitory.

When we got there, he set me down in the parlor for a lecture I should have heard years before. From someone. But never had.

Bill explained to me that few can achieve perfection in many areas. There is not enough time in twenty-four-hour days, nor is there enough strength inside our physical bodies. He shocked me by saying, "To place yourself under the kind of strain of striving for perfection in many areas is useless, silly, and, I believe, wrong!"

I was trying so hard to please God. Surely I hadn't been wrong.

But as we talked that night, I began to see that he was right. I was wrong to impose on my body to the point that I would faint from exhaustion, center stage or anywhere else. I was wrong not to learn more about the uniqueness of the God-created Ruth and understand the majors and the minors He had in mind.

I wish I could explain to you the wonder, the glory, the total utter *joy* of the freedom I found. Alone with God, I understood my majors. I understood my minors. And when someone called me in for a long conference on my responsibility to all my talents, I listened courteously, thanked her for her interest, and walked away, leaving the basket of guilt with her.

There is no superiority.
There is no inferiority.

There are some who think that talents in the creative or performing arts such as painting, sculpture, music, writing, drama, public speaking are of greater value than others. That is nonsense. We saw that when we compared Valerie and her sister. But there are those who believe that if you have any talent in the glamorous public areas, you have a responsibility to make that a major. It is simply *not* true.

So if someone comes along with a basket of guilt for you that because you have a gift for singing, that has to be your life-major and you and God know it is only a "grace note" . . . smile, thank him for his interest, and walk away. Minus the basket of guilt.

There is no superiority.
There is no inferiority.
There is only difference. And each role is of vital importance.
Believe in your own choice made with God's direction.

One of my graduate school chums is now the wife of a politician. In a news interview recently, she was asked if she didn't often feel excluded, alienated, "not a part of" his more glamorous work.

She, the mother of six adopted children, smiled and said, "No. You see, this exuberantly extroverted politician needs a steady quiet center. I provide that. I believe that what he is doing is of greater value than a precise home schedule, so I free him to be gone whenever he has need . . . and when he has need for a haven of loving acceptance, I and the children await."

I loved the last line of that interview. She was quoted as saying, "I freely release him to serve God as he was intended to . . . and I am happy to serve God *the way I was intended to.*" (Italics mine)

This dynamic senator can serve God. His soft-spoken, seldom-seen-in-public wife can serve God. One service is not superior to the other. They are both of value.

No one can make you feel guilt, unless you give them permission. When you know God's leadings, walk freely in the world, head high, heart filled only with joy.

Believe in your choice.

Could You Discipline Yourself in Your Choice?

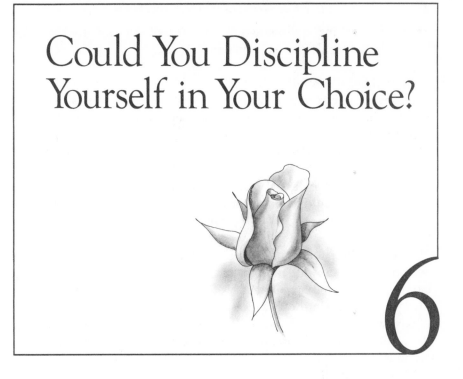

6

When I was a college professor, one of the most frequently written notes on critique sheets to my students was this: "Your talents are God's gift to you. What you do with those talents is your gift to Him."

When you truly understand, with God, His wonderful dream of the one-of-a-kind you, you will know that you are important in our world. You also know that you and God can identify the majors and minors. If others disagree, you can still walk free.

With all of this self-understanding, there is another issue you must clearly face: discipline. This is a sobering thought because it does not come easily and it is an imperative. If you are to "be your best" in the majors of your life, you must be sternly disciplined.

If, as with Janna, you discover that your life-major is a desire to be with people:

- Are you willing to study communication principles?
- Are you willing to learn to focus on the needs of others rather than your own?
- Are you willing to delve into psychological fundamentals of helping?

• Are you willing, beginning now, to refine all skills involved in being the very best "people-person" you can be?

Think about it carefully.

Whatever is the specific of your God-dream, are you willing to give of your energies, your concentration, your disciplined effort to make it become a reality?

God gave you the dream. God gave you the raw abilities to make it come true . . .

> but the development of that dream,
> the cultivation of those abilities . . .
> > are *your responsibility.*

It was one thing for Janna to sit under the tree and contemplate life. It was something totally different for Janna to study, discipline her time and energies, analyze and prepare herself for effectively working with people.

Easy to dream. Hard to make it come true.

So, as we ponder the wonder of the God-created uniqueness of you and all you can be in the future, think seriously about whether you are truly willing to pay the price so that dreaming can become reality.

Don't shrug it off.

It is vital. Now.

Do you remember Caroline, who wrote that her doctorate in music began in a moment of self-insight at age fourteen? I have seen many other fourteen-year-olds who had their moment of understanding. But they never saw that life-dream fulfilled because they were unwilling to sacrifice the pleasure of the present and to work with persistence toward that future goal.

They knew the dream. But they didn't work toward its development. It hung in their lives—unfulfilled—forever.

They didn't understand fully that they were deciding against the life-dream. They just "moved with the tide" and the life-dream slipped away. They walked without concentrated discipline, without fully understanding its importance.

I received a letter recently from a girl who was brilliant in high school chemistry. She won several contests her sophomore year, but by her junior year she had quit giving her best. "Above average" was easy for her. She slipped by without straining for excellence.

The result, of course, was that when applying for college scholarships, she was bypassed. Her parents took out a government loan, but she found that the stiff college competition did not show her off as "above average" as her high school efforts had. She left college the second semester of her freshman year.

Now she writes that she is twice-divorced, working in a clothing store, but has plans to go back to school and become a chemist. Her letter filled me with sadness, because there was frustration in every line.

She knew what was true for herself. She had been unwilling to discipline herself to make the dream come true.

It is so important for you to see the need for discipline in your life. Every day.

Before Caroline won a college scholarship in piano, she worked hard to understand theory, harmony, and technique. She sacrificed many lazy hours at the beach and with the gang at McDonald's in relentless practice at the keyboard.

Before Janet became an expert radio technician, she enmeshed herself in a training program so rigorous that she literally spent some weeks "in her shack" (where her equipment was set up) without leaving it. Her meals were brought in by friends. She slept on a rollaway bed.

Before Sally became the successful homemaker for an active politician and six children, she studied the arts of cooking, sewing, rug making, and getting out blueberry stains! She studied child psychology and seriously filled journals with her strategies on the responsibility of molding young lives.

These three now find the reality of their life-dreams because they disciplined themselves from the moment they understood it was their life-dream. They worked hard to refine their "raw abilities" into glowing useful tools in our world. They made their prayers for dreams-come-true *just.*

The girl who wrote me recently did not make her prayers just. And they now hang, all-unfulfilled, in her unsatisfying life.

The talents that you have are God's gift to you.
What you do with those talents is your gift to Him.
Of what quality will your gift be?
For it to be of finest quality, you must choose the path of discipline. It is not glamorous. But it is the road to personal fulfillment.

Those Answers Can Only Be Chosen by You

7

In many ways, you are, at this moment, in the most important period of your life. Why? Because you are, daily, making choices, both large and small, that determine your entire future.

We've talked about some of the big ones. But there are a lot of little choices you are now making that are forming who you are now and who you will be as a woman.

My mother understood that years ago and she tried to explain it to me in a letter that I still cherish. Its pages are yellow and fragile. But I'd like for you to read it.

When I was eighteen, she wrote:

My dearest young woman,
Clocks steadily tick-tock and tell each hour in its turn. They do not jump eighteen years without notice. Or at least they are not supposed to. And yet it seems so short a time ago you lay against my heart a baby thing.

But now I look over and see you there—the soft light shining on your brown hair—and I know you are no longer a child. You stand on the threshold of life, and all the prizes hang like bags of candy on a Christmas tree, and you can take your choice.

But choices are eternal, little girl.

Choices shape your life.

In these next few years, you will choose what kind of woman you will be. You will choose whether you will meet life with a frown or a smile, whether you will be minutely self-righteous or strong enough to say, "I'm sorry," whether you will live to please yourself or to help others.

Reread that last paragraph. Had you thought that those small choices were forming the who of yourself as a woman? So many times it is easy to forget that these are choices. For whatever reason, we feel "rotten" and so we frown and grumble and are unpleasant to be around. But that is a choice. Had you thought of it that way? You are not the victim of your emotions. You choose to give in to your personal feelings and wear a grouchy frown. Or you have the option of choosing to smile, in spite of personal feelings, and being cheerful and happy. It is a choice and is important in the total who of you in a way different from career choices but, in some ways, even more vital.

You choose self-righteousness or the strength to say "I'm sorry," my mother said long ago. It is so easy to be self-satisfied; it is so hard to look at things as they are, recognize personal error, and take the blame. And it is a choice. Made often. And in that small, but character-forming choice, you determine much of the who of the woman you will be.

My mother's letter continues:

As you face womanhood, you will choose whether you will meet people with harsh criticism and unbending standards or whether you will meet people with your heart whispering:

If I could only see the road you came,
The jagged rocks and crooked way,
I would more kindly think of your mis-steps
And only praise.

If I could know the heartaches you have felt,
The longings for the things that never came,
I would not misconstrue your erring then
Nor even blame.

Perhaps of all choices in our relations with others, *this* is the most important.

It is a choice. A vital one.

You can choose to be critical of others. You can choose to try to understand the why of others. You can choose to be harsh, rigid, unbending. You can choose to be gentle, kind, forgiving. It is a choice.

My brothers and I had a family joke. We used to say, when Mother was ill and had to be placed in a rest home, that if we put her in a cold cabin in the woods alone, she would spend all her time thanking God for the blankets she might find to keep her warm, the beauty of the woods about her, and the extraordinary texture of the logs of the cabin. She would never doubt that we had put her there with purest motive and deepest love.

If that sounds extreme, you would have had to have known my mother. She had spent a lifetime *choosing* to be "gentle, kind, forgiving" so that by the end of her life, her children who knew her best truly believed that the hypothetical example of the cabin in the woods was true!

But the basis of such a positive personality was made in choices daily, sometimes hourly, when she was young. The who of the woman was determined by her decisions as a girl. And as she grew.

She discusses more about this as the letter continues.

As you face womanhood, you will choose the way you will meet storm. For there will be times when all your world will be in violent upheaval. Will you be overcome, or will you stand serene and strong? The choice will be yours. The secret is on whom you *focus:* yourself or others?

"But," you may ask, "what if others have caused the storm? "
What then?

The choice is yours, young woman. Will you choose to be bitter and resentful, or will you choose to be forgiving and forgetful?

"But how can I forget the unkind things that are said, the cruel and unfair treatment that I have received?" you ask.

I only know of one way. Search yourself in the light of the incident and see how you may profit by the pain. Then choose to forget it. Never talk about it, and never think about it. Never speak even to your best friend about it. When it bobs into your mind, banish it at once. It will surprise you how quickly you can forget when you choose to forget.

Because my mother practiced that so fully, her children came up with the family joke of the cabin in the woods. She is the only person I have known in a lifetime that that joke would have fit. I find it (the joke) a supreme tribute to her determined choices and her disciplined use of them.

My mother wrote of other choices.

As you face womanhood, you will choose the way you will meet joy and triumph. For there will be times when life will be a glorious circle. In those moments, will you be grateful or arrogant? Will you be awed or proud? Will you be giving or receiving? The choice is yours.

Had you thought of that as a choice? It is. And you can alienate people forever if you are not careful of how you choose to be a winner!

My mother concluded this letter with a list of important choices about which she was concerned.

As you stand on the threshold of life, and all the prizes hang like bags of candy on a Christmas tree, you must take your choice.

You must *choose* the level of education you will achieve.

You must *choose* the profession you will pursue.

You must *choose* the degree of excellence you will attain.

You must *choose* the man with whom you want to spend the rest of your life.

You must *choose* the kind of woman you will be.

Dearest young woman, as you stand on the threshold of life, all the prizes hang like bags of candy on a Christmas tree and you can take your choice. But remember . . . *choices are eternal.*

I sit here and look at your flowing brown hair, your youthful form, and my heart aches to hold you steady, insist you use my maturity. I want intensely to push you aside, step into your place, and make the choices for you.

My love wants only the highest and the best for you, my child . . . but my love is not enough!

> I know that the world's wintry storms
> Will attack so hard,
> They would blow out
> The candle of your trust,
> Your faith,
> That would guide your choices
> In life.
> But I can give you no certain armor
> Against storm
> Unless
> I learn
> Release.

> My love is not enough.

> But God, too, wants
> Only the highest
> And the best for you.
> My child, place your hand in His.

Here is your armor against storm.
He will guide you to
Life's finest joys.
My love is not enough.
I must release you.
The choices must be yours.

That letter is as relevant to you today as it was to me then. The choices of all the large elements, all the small elements of your becoming a woman, are yours!

What Does It Mean to Be a Woman?

Three

A Prayer for the Young and Lovely

Dear God, I keep praying
    For the things I desire,
You tell me I'm selfish
    And "playing with fire"—
It is hard to believe
    I am selfish and vain,
My desires seem so real
    And my needs seem so sane,
And yet You are wiser
    And Your vision is wide
And You look down on me
    And You see deep inside,
You know it's so easy
    To change and distort,
And things that are evil
    Seem so harmless a sport—
Oh, teach me, dear God,
    To not rush ahead
But to pray for Your guidance
    And to trust You instead,
For You know what I need
    And that I'm only a slave
To the things that I want
    And desire and crave—
Oh, God, in your mercy
    Look down on me now
And see in my heart
    That I love You somehow,
Although in my rashness,
    Impatience and greed
I pray for the things
    That I Want and Don't Need—
And instead of a Crown
    Please send me a Cross
And teach me to know
    That All Gain is but Loss,
And show me the way
    To joy without end,
With You as my Father,
    Redeemer and Friend—
And send me the things
    That are hardest to bear,
And keep me forever
    Safe in Thy care.

HELEN STEINER RICE

Who Are You
as a Female?

I

That wonderful romanticist, Irving Berlin, wrote:

> The girl that I marry will have to be
> As soft and as pink as a nursery;*

That was a very simple answer to the question, "Who am I as a female?" But even if soft pinkness was plausible in the 1940s when this song was written, it is no longer a true definition.

The 1980s saw the first woman become a judge on the Supreme Court. Margaret Thatcher has served as prime minister of Britain. Women have moved into executive positions in various corporations and companies across America. My friend Anne, for example, is president of a computer firm.

The female of today may still be feminine, but the "soft" and "pink" uselessness of the Berlin lyric is outdated. Women are not merely decorative, the world is now admitting; they are vital contributing members to all phases of society.

That notion did not come easily. Until this century, women were not considered "intelligent" enough to vote. But through hardheaded persistence and a lot of work, women have, now, won their place in the world.

But something interesting happens, often, in battles of this nature. In the fighting for equality. it is easy to swing to an extreme position; when the dust dies down, the soldiers have forgotten what they were fighting for.

I believe that has happened with some of our "women's libbers" of today. I think that, in all the confusion of warring for equal rights, many forgot *what it is to be a woman.*

We have gained in the work place. We have lost in self-knowledge.

Many of today's extremists speak of *unisex.* They speak with no basis in logic. Their irresponsible assertions deny one of the most precious of all God-gifts: the wondrous difference between male and female.

Wondrous is an overworked word. I chose it purposefully, however, because I believe it best captures that distinctiveness. It can only be a "wonder" to understand the specific strengths of man, the specific strengths of woman, and how, together, they can face life as a forceful unit.

To deny these "wondrous" differences seems, to me, to be sacrilege. *Who are you as a female?* I present the following declaration and defense:
Declaration: The basic, fundamental instinct of womankind
        is *to be a giver.*
Defense: Uniqueness of gender in three areas:

Biologically, we are created to *give* haven to a growing embryo.
Biologically, we are created to *give* a warm-womb environment to a developing personality.
Biologically, we are created to *give* nourishment to a hungry child.
Therefore, biologically, we are distinctively structured for the purpose of *giving* to another.

Emotionally, we are created to *give* love with special warmth.
Emotionally, we are created to *give* a peculiar aura of joy and peace.
Emotionally, we are created to *give* a steadying source of strength.
Therefore, emotionally, we are distinctively gifted for the purpose of *giving* to another.

Mentally, we are created to *give* a down-to-earth realism men never achieve.
Mentally, we are created (paradoxically) to *give* inspiration.

Mentally, we are created to *give* a wisdom unique to our gender. Therefore, mentally, we are distinctively endowed for the purpose of *giving* to another.

Some may disagree with me. I know that clearly. But here is why I think I am right.

In our recent efforts to be equal with men, much of this unique quality of *giving* has been submerged. Pressured into competing with men, women have overlooked or pushed aside their own basic instincts so their own self-understanding has been blurred.

Pearl Buck, writing in her book *To My Daughters with Love,* asked:

> Do you know who you are? Well, I will tell you. You are a woman . . . You ask what that means? It means that you are a creation entirely different from man . . . [everything] is expressed differently . . . Your love permeates your whole being . . . You see why you must not be ignorant about yourself.
>
> Do not compete with [man], for competition is impossible between you. Neither can lose and neither wins. I deny the battle of the sexes. If we do battle, then the battle is already lost for both. Victory is only to be achieved in unity—victory over life and, yes, over death.
>
> Accept your womanhood, my daughter, and rejoice in it. It is your glory that you are a woman. . . .

Biologically, woman is created to *give.* No one can debate that.

Emotionally, woman is created to *give* in ways that can only come from God-created distinctiveness. Search through history, through all cultures, you will find that woman has always been, indeed shall always be, the pioneer of giving emotional balance—to herself first and, from that reservoir, outpouring to her family, her society, even her world.

Biologically, emotionally, there is a fundamental difference, as Pearl Buck flatly states, between men and women. But it is a difference of kind. Not of reality. Not of degree. Not of quality. Of kind.

The same thing is true of mental attributes. Men, of course, can make great achievements with their minds, just as can women. The difference is in kind.

Man can become totally caught up in adventure and excitement, discovery and creation, exploration for its own sake. This is his arena of activity.

Certainly women become enmeshed in those same things. But there is the basic maternal *giving* instinct that wants not only to adventure, discover, create, explore, and gain insights. This instinct wants to use those things for others. The woman always searches for a way to give from the life-venture. She is never content to master its challenges for the sake of mastery alone.

The American author, H. L. Mencken, wrote in his book *In Defense of Women:*

> Women . . . see at a glance what most men could not see with search-lights and telescopes; [women] are at grips with the essentials of a problem before men have finished debating its externals. [Women] are the supreme realists of the race. Apparently illogical, [women] are the possessors of a rare and subtle super-logic. Apparently whimsical, they hang to the truth with a tenacity which carries them through every phase of its incessant, jelly-like shifting of forms.

God created women with a mental capacity that is distinctively structured for perceiving, understanding, coping . . . and *giving* to those about her.

Who are you as a female?

You are uniquely a giver.

How Do You Learn About Love?

2

When I was fourteen, I fell head over heels in love. He was tall, dark, and handsome. When he smiled, my heart did flip-flops with such force I could hardly breathe.

One of our neighbors was a kindly older woman who found my emotions delightful. She laughed at my assertions that this was for real. "It's only puppy love," she would tell me. "It won't last. Not with this young man. Probably not with many others. You have to grow up to know about real love."

She would giggle as she remembered when she was fourteen. "My father would talk to me then just as I'm talking to you now. 'Don't throw your hat over the windmill,' he'd say. 'You're going to need it for the feller who next passes by!' "

I didn't understand then why her teasing made me feel humiliated and silly. As I look back, I think I know.

She was right. My "love" for this young man did not last forever. I should not have "thrown my hat over the windmill," as her father phrased it, because there were many other young men for whom I would want to "wear my hat" before I made a final choice. So she was right in that appraisal.

But in her degrading "young love" with the label "puppy love," I think she was wrong. The label makes it seem foolish and ridiculous, and it is not. For young love is a vital, imperative, growing experience.

Until that time, I had been a child only. *Being loved* was my major concern. Falling in love with this tall, dark, handsome young man at age fourteen was the beginning of my heart's turning outward, away from self, focusing on another. This was the first opening of my spirit to give love to someone else. Ultimately, I would have the capacity to give first place to another human being: my husband.

That growing, opening, flowering process did take many years. As my neighbor-friend predicted, there were many "wonderful" boys who were part of it. But it all began when I was fourteen with this one who was "tall, dark, and handsome!"

I believe that initial giving to another deserves more dignity, however, than my friend's label, "puppy love." It was a beautiful and important maturing period for me. It was the first pushing out of the boundaries of my heart. It was the first thrusting forth of my spirit. It was the first reaching, on my own, to find, accept, grasp responsibility. For real love is responsibility and it must grow and develop as do all vital elements of character.

Gradually, through all my dating experiences, through all the lessons learned in maturing from one "great love" to another, my heart surpassed the demand only to be loved and developed the capacity of focusing chiefly on giving love until, ultimately, I was ready for the demands of true love and marriage.

Demands? Yes. Marriage is responsibility. Marriage is being able to say, "I am responsible *for* and *to* you."

A child cannot understand that. That is why it takes a woman, fully grown, to be ready for marriage.

It's easy to get caught in the excitement of being loved. Any child can be happy then. It is adult-demanding to give love and say, "I am responsible for and to you. Forever." Only an adult can qualify.

I remember when I reached that moment.

Bill and I had been seriously dating for many months. But he knew the strain I felt to live up to other peoples' goals for me. He knew that I had never come to grips with what was the most true dream for Ruth.

I listened too much to outside voices. I was too anxious to please others. I was easily swayed by the demands that I follow others' guidelines for me, walk this or that career path—I had been too pressured to be extraordinary.

One afternoon, a professional lady who was impressed with my potential called me to her office. She told me what a nice young man Bill was and she approved of our dating. After graduation, Bill would leave college to enter the pastorate; he might ask me to go with him, she said.

She warned me that such a decision on my part would ruin my life. She graphically described the careers that could be mine. She pleaded with me to delay thoughts of love and marriage for years. Gain degrees; gain expertise in your careers; and then think of marriage. This was her advice.

I left her office in a deeply reflective mood. I walked slowly across campus and up the stairs to my dormitory room. My roommate had been there and left the college paper spread open on the bed. It displayed the photographs of those who had made *Who's Who in American Colleges and Universities* that year. It was an honor for juniors and seniors.

I was a freshman, but as I perused the pages, I understood that, in a couple of years, my photograph could appear there. I knew the pride it would bring to the lady who had just counseled me. I knew the fulfillment it would bring to everyone in my life.

Except me!

And, in a sudden bursting moment, I fell on my knees beside the bed, buried my face in the paper, and began to sob, "O God! You know that although there are many talents I would like to develop—many careers in which I could achieve—what *I* want most in all the world is to be a wife and mother. O dear God, You know this has been my high and holy dream since my first memory."

I grabbed a Kleenex and stood to walk to the window. I looked out at the beauty of the campus, the bright blur of colors as students went about their affairs. I turned back to look at the open newspaper and cried: "O dear, dear God who created me, You know that I love Bill. I want to go to his parsonage with him. I want to make his home, cook his meals, care for him, work with him, create new lives with him. O God! *This* is my most high and holy dream."

I stood very still. I had been declaiming, pleading with intensity. Now my shoulders huddled into submission, and I whispered softly, "Is it all right that this is my most precious dream?"

And, deep inside where the meanings are, I knew my Creator whispered, "It's all right. I created you with this as your true dream." I felt as if He were smiling as I understood, "It is all right for you to be Ruth."

I wept in relief as peace filled my being. Then I was still for a long time.

I knew what this decision meant.

I would have to take a stand that most of the people of my world would call young, foolish, and unwilling to serve God with my talents. I shrank from that barrage. But I knew that I had now, finally, discovered with my

Creator that what was true for me was the high and holy dream of love and marriage—and it was all right.

Because I knew that, I knew I could refuse the guilt that would be handed to me. I would walk, with head high, and "reach my unreachable star."

After a long while, I leaned over and folded the open paper. With that action, I surrendered my place in *Who's Who in American Colleges and Universities* in the next two years, at least. I washed my face and repaired my makeup. I brushed my hair and then called Bill.

We met in our favorite spot, under some giant trees where we sat on the grass together. I told him of the afternoon's experiences.

He listened, watching me carefully. His eyes searched me out. I knew his heart was exploring my own; his mind was assessing my words.

When I was all through, there was a warm, waiting, healing silence. Then he took my hands in his and said, "You grew up today. You reached for your *own* dream."

He tilted my chin, his eyes brimming with loving joy, and he said huskily, "Now you are ready to be a wife. *My* wife."

My heart soared like a kite, almost lifting me off the ground. It was the dreamed-of moment, when everything was filled with beauty, awe, worship.

That is "How *I* Learned About Love." And I believe it is, for the most part, typical of the learning process for all.

It began at age fourteen with the pushing out of heart-boundaries to include another person. It expanded through other male–female relationships as the joy of being loved was gradually superseded by the happiness of giving love. Ultimately, when I was mature enough for responsibility, my most high and holy dream came true. A young man offered me his love, his name, his life. I accepted.

And on a glowing St. Valentine's night, in a gown of white satin and lace, the organ played Mendelssohn and I became Bill's bride. Marriage was my best dream come true.

It was then. Has ever been. Shall ever be.

I never regretted it. It was true for me.

When Bill went to his first parish as a young minister, I went with him. All three of my educational degrees came after marriage. All of my career achievements came after marriage. Today I am listed in more *Who's Who* books than I have taken time to count.

Those things have been splendid and exciting. They have proven that all the "majors" I had been given by God were fulfilled. But in deeply earnest prayer in a dormitory room on a college campus, I found what was *the major* in the uniqueness of the who of Ruth. And in "giving my best" to love and marriage, I have found my greatest joy.

This is only my personal experience.

I am *not* advocating that an early marriage is always best. I am *not* asserting that one can always finish three degrees and form multiple careers along with marriage. I am *not* generalizing in any way from my one personal experience.

But I think it may be time for someone to stand up and say, *"This is possible!"*

My mail is now filled with letters from young women who are in a panic because they yearn for love and marriage but the majority of voices are saying, "Wait!" I hear it constantly on radio and television talk shows; read it in magazines and books. I know it in my personal realm.

Only recently, a woman wrote me in despair because her daughter wanted to marry early. "I did that," wrote her mother, "and the marriage was a disaster. I tell her she *has* to wait until she has finished her education, found a secure place in her career, understands all about life, and then she will know how to choose a marriage partner. *If she marries this young, I know from experience, that she will ruin her life!"*

That woman, as most of mass media today, is generalizing. I, however, could paraphrase her and say, *"If she marries this young, I know from experience, that she will have a glorious life of fulfillment!"*

This woman and many others are generalizing from their personal events. Were I to make that paraphrase, I would be generalizing from *my* personal events. But one generalization is as invalid as another. Neither is adequate.

The point I want to make is that no one else can know who you are, who your young man is, or what you and he will make of life together. You don't know for sure either. But if you are both close to God, you are in a better position to make that decision than anyone else.

What you must do is know that what is best for one is not necessarily best for another. The woman who married young and found it "a disaster" can*not* know that will be true for her daughter. I who married young and found it "majestic" can*not* know that will be true for my son.

My mother wrote to me when I was eighteen the letter contained in an earlier chapter. There is a concept that fits here.

She said, "My heart aches to . . . insist you use my maturity. I want intensely to push you aside, step into your place, and make the choices for you . . . But my love is not enough. I must release you. The choices must be yours."

There is the key. "The choices must be yours."

Only you can know what is true for you. But when you know, follow God's inner leadings. Do not be swayed by exterior voices. No one else can know *what* is best for you. No one else can know *when* is best for you. No one can know except you and God.

Deep in the heart of every woman I have known well, love and marriage has been the important dream. Sometimes on talk shows or in magazine articles, women assert that they have never had, have not now, and shall never have such a desire. I cannot know the truth of their statements. I can only listen to or read their words.

But I have counseled hundreds of women across our nation, and when we have talked deeply and honestly, each, without exception, has told me that love and marriage has always been her most high and holy dream. It has not come true for all of them.

Because it has not come true, some have, publicly, tried to deny that the dream exists. But when engaged in deeply personal sharing, I have never talked with a woman who did not admit the dream.

In our call for women's rights to have careers other than love and marriage, a defensiveness seems to have developed that causes many women to proclaim they only want to live with and for themselves. That may or may not be true. I cannot know about them. But if the dream is true for you, remain honest about it. Refuse the posture of defensiveness in your life.

There are speeches, books, articles, entire magazines devoted to the joys and adventures of single bliss. I'm sure a majority of these are true. I have many friends who have found profound fulfillment and genuine happiness without a man. They have made homes, created beauty, found and met challenge, given lavishly to the world. But I believe it has taken an extra supply of courage, strength, and fortitude. I salute them.

For there is always that one empty space in the heart: the knowledge that, no matter how exciting is their world, the dream of love, marriage, children didn't come true.

There are so many reasons why it may be so. One of my single friends, for family reasons, went to a different college every year for four years so she was never able to establish long-lasting relationships. Immediately upon graduation, she was given a fabulous job as a roving reporter. Today she adventures all over the United States and abroad for stories for television.

She shares the joy of my marriage and children and then, often, ruefully says, "It just never worked out for me. There were some that might have been right, but I had to move on too quickly to know for sure. Maybe someday . . ."

And we both pray a secret prayer.

She has a life of fulfillment, success, joy, challenge; she has many friends of both sexes; she is contributing to the betterment of our world in a very special way. But it never worked out in her life, as it did in mine, that a young man said, "You are now ready to be a wife. My wife."

But she does not deny the dream.

And I admire her for that.

She is honest about a dream placed in most, if not all, hearts of girls who grow to be women. Some recent extremists have made single women feel shame in admitting that they would choose marriage at all were it possible in their situation. I find that sad.

Make your decision now. If you have the dream, be true to it. When you wish on an evening star, when you pray, even when you talk with other people, don't be ashamed to admit the dream.

It is nothing of which to be ashamed.

My friend says, for her, she never married probably because she was never in one place long enough. Another friend became head of a savings and loan business when her father died suddenly, and there has never been time to get to know anyone outside of her immediate work place. Another friend is so shy that she has never said more than two connected words to a male in her lifetime. The reasons continue. But whatever the specific, it doesn't matter really.

The dream didn't happen. Yet.

My mother was an "old-maid schoolteacher" for years in the era when it was truly scandalous! When she talked about it later, she would get a certain dreamy look in her eyes and say, "I just always knew there would be someone, someone who rose above all the others." And then she would smile. I, the child, would sit in the quietness of her happy memories and think of the excitement she must have felt when that dynamic young preacher strode into her life.

She had played the piano for many of his revivals and camp meetings. She had not known that he had even noticed her. But he had. And although it was years after most of her friends were married with families, she finally found that "someone who rose above all the others," and her dreams of love and marriage became realities.

Decide now that you will not join the extremists in denying the dream. Decide now that, whether or not it comes true for you, it is your dream. I believe that self-honesty is vitally important.

It gives you the freedom to wholly admit who you are. Be who you are, and revel in the beauties of the dream. And, then, if it does come to you, you can claim it as one of God's truly most divine gifts.

What About Sex in the Twentieth Century?

3

I am going to begin my answer to that question from another era. I cannot cite the exact year because I don't know it. But when I was thirteen, my mother took a carefully folded clipping from a Sunday school paper out of her Bible (where she saved Most Important Papers), sat me down, and read the following article by Connie Moore Hunt.

> When I was thirteen, my mother took a carefully folded newspaper clipping from a drawer of the buffet in the dining room. She unfolded it and read me every word about the story of the two fruit stores. Maybe your mother has read or told it to you.
>
> The two fruit stores were utterly different. In one, the fruit was put on a counter near the sidewalk where all who passed would most certainly know it was there. People who cared to might pick it up, handle it, even taste a grape to see how good it was. There was an intermittent buzz of flies about the place, but the fruit could always be washed when one got home. No one seemed to mind anyhow. People were always walking by and admiring the fruit. It was a most popular place. And at night there was no one to see how much of the worn, pinched fruit the owner threw away.
>
> Tony (I believe that was really the man's name in the newspaper clipping) had the other store. The fruit in it was kept behind glass. Through

the glass you could see fresh drops of water still glistening on the bunches of grapes. When people pointed out to Tony what they wanted to buy and take home, he would carefully take out the fruit on white sheets of paper, place it in a sack, and hand it to the customer.

"Nobody," mother said as she folded the clipping back again, "wants to buy fruit handled and bruised and spoiled. People who want choice fruit buy the kind that is fresh and untouched." She said a lot more then and cried a little, I remember. I was impressed and made solemn promises and knew that there were things I must always refuse to do. It was a long time after that that I realized the purpose of refusing was not just to keep myself clean and good, but was also to allow myself eventually to grow into womanhood, to become ultimately, wifely material.

It's so easy to feel, when we are trying to live up to our ideals, that we are merely putting ourselves in glass cases while everyone walks by not even noticing us but admiring the fruit that is out by the sidewalk. We almost forget that someone who really cares will come inside, point us out, ask for us, and carefully take us home.

I believe that when God created you as a female being, He instilled within you a yearning for physical purity. I believe it is basic to want to save yourself for the forever-love of your life.

I know many violently, vehemently disagree.

From situation comedies to magazines to books, mass media is hounding twentieth-century America with the advice to "Do what you want to when you want to with whom you want to." In spite of this "new morality," I am convinced it is anathema to every instinct of womanhood.

I have kept prolific journals since childhood. The entry describing my emotions following my marriage begins with this poem:

> Between the covers of this book
> We keep the golden past
> When we were a radiant bride and groom
> And the world was ours at last . . .
> And every season, each in turn,
> That saw our joy and pain . . .
> A record of our sunshine bright . . .
> And a record of our rain . . .

The poem is lengthy, but the first quatrains set the tone. It is, indeed, what the title calls it: "A Record of Love."

I had bought a negligee for each night of our first week together. I saved them to wear on our silver anniversary week. And I did. All seven. They all fit; they were all still lovely.

But of that very first night, I wrote in this journal:

Bill and I had planned the night in detail. I dressed in the bathroom; he in the bedroom. I wanted the luxury of dressing for an impressive "entrance."

I buried my face in the creamy negligee before I slipped it over my body. I fixed my hair and adjusted everything just so. I looked in the mirror: it was *me! Ruth!* Not someone in a fairy tale; not someone in a movie; not even my best friend.

I was a bride!

Taking a deep breath, I walked into the bedroom. Bill was putting something in a drawer and as he turned, he saw me. He just stood, like he was mesmerized, and in a rush of words, he said, "Oh my! You're so beautiful!"

It was a fantastic moment. And we both just stood there, relishing it.

We had agreed to repeat our memorized wedding vows at our bedside that night before our first prayer together. And we did. In tears. In kisses. In forever promises.

And then we went to bed as husband and wife. And when he touched me, my body came alive . . . as if it had never been alive before . . . as if it had been asleep and was suddenly awakened to throbbing vibrancy. *I know how to say what it was like!* It was like Galatea, in the Greek myth. I, who had been marble, was turned to flesh at his kiss. It was a kind of miracle! And just think: it is mine . . . ours . . . forever!

For months, our hearts have been one. Last night, our bodies became one. There is no description I can find.

Can glory be put into words? Can roaring excitement be explained? Can whirlwinding joy be expressed? Can married unity be put on paper? Never! Never in a thousand years!

But it can be experienced in every corpuscle of body, mind and soul. And it is ours! It is ours! I can only say, "Thank You, God! This sexual oneness is a miracle above miracles! Thank You, God!"

I received a letter recently from a young woman asking me to tell her any arguments I might have why she should "save herself" for the commitment of marriage. She wrote me a twenty-page dissertation about why she felt she should have "freedom of expression in a car, in a motel, under a tree. Wherever the urge comes," she asserted, "I feel that self-denial is not only unnecessary deprivation but can be damaging in its restraint."

I made no formal reply to her arguments as she had expected. Instead, I simply Xeroxed these paragraphs from the fragile, yellowed, breaking sheets of my personal journal. Underneath, I penned in longhand, "It is that 'miracle above miracles' I want to be yours . . . forever!"

In response, she sent me a bound copy of the story of Galatea. Scrawled on the front page were these words: "I understand. It *is* the miracle I want. It is worth waiting for. I see that if you let everybody do it just anywhere, anytime, just fooling around, you know . . . well, then, the miracle never happens. There just *isn't any miracle!*

"Yes. It's the miracle I want."

And it was "the miracle" that Connie Moore Hunt's mother wanted for her daughter when she read the newspaper clipping about the fruit stores to her when she was thirteen. It was "the miracle" my mother wanted for me when she read me the same story. It is the same "miracle above miracles" that I want for you and that you want for yourself as we, in twentieth-century enlightenment, talk about the meaning of sex. It is "the miracle" we want: the miracle of love everlasting, love creative, love blooming into a home, children, and a whole wonderful new world.

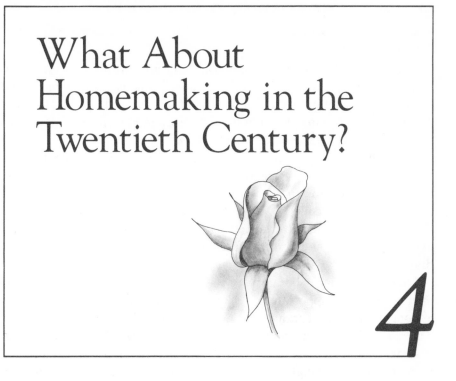

What About Homemaking in the Twentieth Century?

Homemaking, in any century, is life's greatest adventure.

In an article entitled "A Different Sort of Liberation," Washington reporter, Carolyn Lewis, wrote in *The New York Times:*

> In our eagerness to exact equal treatment [with men], we women seem to be forgetting who we are. We are not men. Men cannot bear children. And for a woman, the birth of a child is a transforming experience.
>
> Of course, it's great to write speeches for a Senator, or design public policy for an education department, or work as an administrative assistant to a high-powered executive—but all of that can pale dramatically before the tender wonder of a newborn living creature.
>
> Here is a tiny, talcumed ball of potential, the whole luminous future of the universe, waiting to be loved and shaped. There is nothing either inconsequential or demeaning about choosing this child as one's life work.
>
> Nor is there anything shameful in wanting to make life comfortable and happy for another adult human, like a husband. There are good and important things to do inside the home, and the women's movement makes light of that fact at its peril.

Loving a man, creating with him new lives—homemaking—is a demanding job.

What does it ask of you?

Service.

Pearl Buck wrote to her daughters: "You are fortunate in the many ways you have of expressing love. To arrange his house, to plan his meals, to care for his comfort, to serve him—yes, I insist upon the word, for such service is sacred to love, even in the simplest and most menial ways. Menial? Nothing is menial where there is love."

It is fashionable these days to sneer at the rewards of love-service. But when you truly love someone, is there a more basic yearning than to give, to create a haven, to serve?

I have taught in college, written books and plays. I can assure you that there is no fulfillment to compare with making a home. From personal experience, I am convinced that learning to bake a cake, learning to make drapes, learning to arrange flowers can be high adventure!

There is no office, laboratory, or stage that offers as many creative avenues or executive opportunities as homemaking. The household drudge is a woman who hasn't trained for her career and does not understand it. The perceptive person who has taken the time to learn how to be creative in cooking, sewing, and decorating knows that the necessary routines of homemaking are a small fraction of the whole. Sweeping and dusting are no more tedious than filing or answering correspondence. In fact, those duties are deeply rewarding, in their own way, because both sweeping and dusting are creative ways of making life more beautiful and comfortable for the one you love.

I found, when running several careers simultaneously, that when I hired someone to do the cooking and housecleaning for my home, I felt an acute sense of loss. I hurried to rearrange my priorities so that I could reassume the "nuts and bolts" parts of home-creation.

I insisted on it. Because I quickly learned that homemaking is more involved than strolling in and out of a well run-house! It is the actual creation, the actual homemaking that gives the house the warmth and wonder of a real home.

Carolyn Lewis wrote: "I'm glad today's woman can pursue a career free of stigma, if that's what she wants to do. But the world outside the home is not the only real world. The only rewards worth having are not necessarily the rewards of salary and status. There are psychic returns in giving and receiving love, in molding a child's mind and spirit . . . [We need to be reminded] of what being a woman can be all about."

The simplest examples for you to consider are the happily married women you know. If there is anything that brings greater joy to most women than to love and live for one man who does the same for you . . .

and, with him, to create new lives and a new home . . . mankind has not found it!

In recent weeks, I have been perusing my own life.

During the years, I have flown about the nation to give speeches to thunderous applause; I have both acted in and directed dramas that played to full houses; I have written books and plays that have circulated throughout the world; I have done scholarly research that has brought raves from the academic community. Yet I truly believe that the only work of lasting significance that I have done has been in my homemaking.

My speeches have long been forgotten; the dramas have slipped into oblivion; the books and plays will go out of print; the research will become outdated. But the two sons Bill and I have created and the home environment we have made for them will go on—into the future—a living testimony to ourselves, to our love.

In *Sixpence in Her Shoe,* Phyllis McGinley wrote:

> Nobody has so far received a Pulitzer Prize for contriving a poetic boiled custard, in spite of the fact (which I know from experience) that it is a feat less easy to perform than writing a ballade. The Nobel Committee has yet to award any laurels to a woman simply for making her home a place of such peace and delight that her family rightfully rise up and call her blessed—if such an odd notion ever occurred to them. . . .
>
> It encourages me to remember that I belong to such an old and continuous company . . . On us rests the burden (and the glory) of seeing to it that the pot boils, the table is set, the sheets get changed, the babies remain healthy, a light shines in the window after dark, and there is refreshment for body and soul waiting at the day's end. . . .
>
> We crave light and warmth in this century. Only the mother, the wife, can supply it for the home. To be a housewife is not easy. Ours is a difficult, a wrenching, sometimes an ungrateful job if it is looked on only as a job. Regarded as a profession, it is the noblest as it is the most ancient in the catalog. Let none persuade us differently or the world is lost indeed.

What about homemaking in the twentieth century?

It is life's greatest adventure; life's noblest profession.

What Does It Mean to Be a Liberated Woman?

Four

The Joy of Unselfish Giving

Time is not measured
   by the years that you live
But by the deeds that you do
   and the joy that you give—
And each day as it comes
   brings a chance to each one
To love to the fullest,
   leaving nothing undone
That would brighten the life
   or lighten the load
Of some weary traveler
   lost on Life's Road—
So what does it matter
   how long we may live
If as long as we live
   we unselfishly give?

HELEN STEINER RICE

What Can the New Freedom Mean to You?

I

"I've Gotta Be Me!" asserted a song of the late sixties. It articulated the thesis that is still very popular: one must have total freedom for selfish impulses to be happy.

There is, of course, a soundness in the inherent philosophy that one must be true to self, accept self, respect self. We've discussed that and we both applaud it as virtue.

But the song and the prevailing ideology springing from it, even today, strains that sound philosophy into simple selfishness. Women have gained much in recent years. But this song makes the sad point that these hard-won prizes for women are inadequate because we have not yet understood them. The leaders of the women's movement have been content to demand freedom. They have not gone on to consider how that freedom can best be used.

The magazine *Mademoiselle* devoted a large portion of one of its issues a few years ago to essays written by young women graduating from college that year. The editors felt that these people would have experienced their campus years as "liberated women" and would be able to report to the nation on what freedom meant to them personally.

One of the authors was Lisa Scwarzbaum who wrote, "College is where everything from high school is undone, where all of one's values . . . are turned topsy-turvy . . . you couldn't help it really. Bombarded daily—and nightly—by thoughts, beliefs, books and sticky-situations-of-the-month your mother never taught you about, what else was there to do but wallow in liberated confusion?"

Liberated confusion.

For many young women those two words succinctly answer the question: What can the new liberation mean to you?

As never before in history, women are free to explore and satisfy justifiable potentials, opportunities, needs, hungers. But too often, they have no idea how to handle all that freedom and so they "wallow in liberated confusion."

Many women dash about throwing themselves into causes and careers, straining every fiber to be free and fulfilled. The fallacy lies in the fact that, in the strained rush of many lives today, free and fulfilled are opposite ends of the pole. Certainly, they are not synonymous.

One of my students almost died from an overdose of sleeping pills when I was a professor. When she was awake, aware, lucid, I asked my burning question, "Why?"

She was one of the brightest minds I had known. She had so much potential she could meet dozens of exciting challenges in her future life. And she was free to pursue whatever she found as her God-created "major" dream.

Yet she had wanted to die. I could not imagine why.

This is what she told me, "Inside, I feel empty. I do a lot of rushing around to classes, activities, training programs . . . but inside, I don't know why. Everyone tells me how terrific my life is and shall be . . . and I smile and do as I am told . . . but inside . . . inside . . ." and the tears flooded as she whispered "inside there is no understanding of me, God . . . or really anything!"

What can the new freedom mean to you?

To my brilliant student, as to Lisa Scwarzbaum and many others, it meant "liberated confusion."

In a sense, women in other times were freer to find fulfillment than we are today. That is true because the force of society did not fragment them, as ours can today. Instead the force of society limited their parameters so tightly that they gained inner stability as a matter of course. Seclusion in the home gave them time to learn about self without even noticing. In simple farm life, away from crowds and noise, they nourished their spirit so that "inside" there was deep understanding of self, God, and many things that my student had been too busy "rushing around" to find. In that era, there was time for "filling" one's mind and heart, even with simple things, so that there was never the feeling of emptiness that made my young friend want to end her life.

To prove that point, I pulled out some of my mother's journals. I have prolific writings from her pen since she was sixteen in 1909. To illustrate the spirit-nourishment possible in that era of little or no liberation for women, read one of her journal entries.

> I have been watching two birds this spring. I heard them calling; watched them mating and building their nest. When the eggs were laid, they took turns sitting on them. When the eggs hatched, I was so excited, I had my whole family come to see the new babies.
>
> The parent birds were busy all spring dropping food into the nest. And when the young ones weren't eating, they sat up and waved their wings; it was such fun to watch them. It was a kind of noise like bumblebees make when they buzzed their wings, exercising them to be ready for their first flight when the time came. Today, the parents and they seemed to have a conference. I was very still as I watched . . . and all of a sudden, one of the young birds flexed its wings and flew away—up, up, up into the azure sky until it was lost from view. I looked back into the nest—and while I had been watching the first flight, all of the others had followed and only the parents sat there—alone now—watching, with me, the specks on the horizon. Their children were gone to find their own worlds. I cried. I couldn't help it because I knew that, one day, soon, I will leave the home my parents have made for me and will have to try my wings alone. I pray I will be as strong in flight as these little birds seemed to be. I pray I will be ready to fly to places of beauty and one day build my own nest for little ones who will be my own.

Later in the journal, she wrote, "On June 22, 1909, I prayed for guidance when I, like the little birds, use my own wings. I am so thankful that I know my prayers were heard and answered. Oh, nothing wonderful has happened to prove it, just a growing certainty and so I wanted to write now: This is April 12, 1910, and I know I can trust in God wherever I go."

At sixteen and seventeen, my mother, in her simple farm life, was quietly learning of self and gaining a faith in God that held through a lifetime.

I don't say that was the "Golden Era" and we should all return to small farms and spend our time watching birds. That would deny us all of the adventures of television, the challenge of moonships, and the use of electric typewriters. The boundaries for women in the early twentieth century were too narrow. Freedom to stretch themselves was denied in too many ways.

But women of that time did have the freedom for self-knowledge, the study of nature, the forming of faith. And as I peruse all of my mother's writings, indeed as I study all of history concerning women of other eras, I wonder if they did not, often, find fulfillment in greater degree than do some of us today who know so little of stillness, who know so little of the workings of God's world, who know so little of our inner thoughts.

One of my students left me breathless the day she described her schedule to me. She was carrying a full academic load in college, taking tennis lessons, teaching piano lessons, directing a children's theater group, and had a part-time job in a law office. When she was alone to wash her hair or iron her clothes, she had the stereo going full-blast because she was an avid fan of rock music. She was surely making full use of her freedom. But she was almost frantic in her pace.

As we talked, she admitted that she was really flaunting her freedom; there was no time for self-exploration; no quiet for soul-contemplation; no stillness for prayer. She said thoughtfully, "Even when I do have time alone, my first impulse is to turn on the stereo. I spend little, really no time just thinking."

I was so impressed with her next statement that I jotted it down on a pad on my desk. "I have only superficial things to give . . . I have only superficial things to be . . . because I never have time to grow myself."

I compared her life with that of my mother. One was in constant motion; she never spent time in silence, just thinking. The other had time to watch the life cycles of birds in the wild, being "very still" as she compared them to life cycles in her own life and praying for divine help to be "strong in flight" so that she, too, could "fly to places of beauty and one day build [her] own nest for little ones of [her] own."

My student was "liberated" so she had the freedom to become the who she chose to be. My mother did not have that freedom, but she found deep fulfillment in understanding life and having time to reach for God.

What could the new freedom mean to you?

It could mean running in meaningless circles as it did for my student who tried to commit suicide. It could mean "superficiality" as it did for the busy young woman who found no "time to grow." It could mean "liberated confusion."

But it doesn't have to.

It can mean freedom for greatness in dimensions never permitted to women before. It can mean quality giving that supersedes the "soft" and "pink" decorative uselessness Irving Berlin's generation gave to women. It could mean profound creativity on pathways newly opened for you.

What could the new freedom mean to you?
It is a matter of personal choice.
Only you can decide. With God.

What Should the New Freedom Mean to You?

One sunny afternoon, I was at work in my college office when an attractive, slender, young lady entered. After our greetings, she flung herself in the big chair across from my desk, looked me over candidly, and then pronounced, "I'm bored! Everything about life bores me. There is simply nothing I can find worth doing. Nothing turns me on anymore!"

I said, "Well, have you considered joining the College Clowns? It's a group who gets in full costume, makeup, the whole bit and spends an entire afternoon doing funny routines at children's wards in nearby hospitals."

She withered me in a glance. "Why would I want to do such a thing? What would it possibly have to offer me?"

"Well," I countered, "we are trying to form a group who will deliver birthday cakes from the church to the elderly on their special day. Would you be interested in helping with that?"

She stood to her feet.

"Look, Professor," she said coldly, "I didn't come here for any do-good suggestions. I am not interested in sick kids or in old people who couldn't hear me if I tried to talk to them! I am interested in something that would be a challenge to *me*. I've been thinking of sky-diving. What do you think?"

I told her I thought it would be fun. I wished her well. She left my office, never to return.

I was, obviously, not "her kind" of person!

There are two kinds of people in the world.

First: There are those who are wrapped up in themselves with no time for others.

Second: There are those who take time and energy to be interested in others.

The first may be called the *Here I am!* kind of person. The latter may be called the *There you are!* kind of person.

The call of the sixties that still shrilly rings through our nation is: Focus on here I am! The world should move and turn on one's own whim and to make self happy.

The girl in my office was answering that call.

Those who break rules, those who take dares in drinking, smoking, drugs, those who go about the world in the sloppiest dress with dirty, mangled hair are those who are centered on self.

"Here I am!" they say. "I shall do my thing regardless of how it affects anyone else—even regardless of how it affects me in the future.

"I want self-gratification now. I will have it at any cost."

In the *Mademoiselle* issue where graduating college women were asked to evaluate the freedom they had been given in college, Gretchen Kuz specifically zeroed in on sexual freedom. The older generation who had limits in this area were convinced that the collegians with liberation were going to be the world's happiest people.

Bravely determining to prove the point, Gretchen and her peers accepted total liberties. They found it drab, dreary, disappointing. In "Sexual Freedom: Is It Worth the Hassle?" she tells of her first sexual experience after entering the freedom of college: "The most positive description I could use to label the exchange would be 'dull.' It was void of emotion, or perhaps, any trace of emotion was deftly disguised as avant-garde nonchalance. I soon found this cool and detached approach characteristic of any future encounters . . .

"And now, two-and-one-half well-seasoned years later, I must admit it's hardly what it's cracked up to be."

She quotes a friend who said, "I finally stopped messing around when I realized that sex is no good unless there is true trust and love involved. Without it, it's just not worth the hassle."

Responding to that quote, Gretchen wrote, "Love and trust—the key words describing exactly what is lacking when college students take their turn at sexual liberation. And after too many disappointing efforts, until we become sick, tired, and disillusioned, we retreat to the tried and true prerequisites of love and trust."

There are more important things than freedom, these collegians discovered. "Love and trust" are far greater in value than liberty from restraints. Selfishness is not the happy way to live.

Gretchen wrote, "Just what drives us, as supposedly intelligent people, to keep banging our heads against the wall? . . . With all this fuss about sexual freedom, I suppose it's hard to stand up and admit it's not what everyone imagines, especially to an anxious world that refuses to let the subject die. Consequently here we sit, tight-lipped and too embarrassed to say we couldn't find [joy in total sexual freedom] . . . Perhaps we could set the record straight—by saying that without love and trust, it's just not worth the hassle."

Of course.

That is why one of the Ten Commandments reads, "Thou shalt not commit adultery." It is a fundamental of our creation. Sexual freedom can never bring joy. Why? Because there are more important things than freedom!

In the last chapter, I gave examples of two of my college students who came to that conclusion. With all the freedom to develop their futures as they chose, they felt an inner emptiness; they were unable to find the road to personal fulfilling growth. And without those ingredients, they found that life itself was "just not worth the hassle." One wanted to quit school; the other tried to die. Why? Because there are more important things than freedom!

Lisa Scwarzbaum, in her essay in *Mademoiselle,* understood that when she called life with too much freedom "liberated confusion." "What could be more important than freedom?" ask the bewildered fighters for liberation. Lisa chose to form a part of the answer to that question in her concluding statement. To do so, she chose a very old list.

She wrote, "For easy reference, then, are the 12 points of the Boy Scout Law: trustworthy, loyal, helpful, friendly, courteous, kind, obedient, cheerful, thrifty, brave, clean and reverent. Sir Robert Baden Powell had the right idea."

It seems clear that although woman has gained mechanically in the past generation, spiritually she has lost. How can that be changed? How can you handle all that freedom best?

In the beginning of this chapter, I identified two kinds of people. We discussed the *Here I am!* person in some detail.

The second group—those who are the *There you are!* people—are the ones who use their freedom with greatest finesse and find the deepest fulfillment in life.

Sir Robert Baden Powell listed twelve characteristics of the *There you are!* person. Lisa Scwarzbaum knew he was from another generation, but she decided he was a very smart man with important clues for today's liberated woman.

On November 20, 1917, my mother copied the following into her journal:

> I expect to pass through this world but once; any good things therefore that I can do, or any kindness that I can show to any fellow creature, let me do it now; let me not defer or neglect it, for I shall not pass this way again.

This was the carefully considered, deliberately written-down code for her life as a young woman. And, even in the limited parameters of her era, she had freedom to find deep, personal fulfillment as a remarkable *There you are!* kind of person.

What should the new liberation mean to you?

It should mean freedom to know self . . . to know God . . . to develop into a *There you are!* kind of person in dimensions and areas never open to women before.

It should mean the freedom to be the most beautiful you.

How Can You Use This New Liberation Best?

How do you handle freedom so that it does not degenerate into "liberated confusion," self-gratification "not worth the hassle," and an empty meaningless life? Open yourself to the freedom of having God direct your life.

My brother is now a colonel in the United States Army. But he will tell you that his greatest days of freedom were when he was a buck private. He didn't have a responsibility in the world—except to obey. He has said he didn't have to think. He was told what to do, when, where, and how. He was totally free of responsibility.

We can have that kind of freedom, and the peace it brings, when we allow God to direct our lives.

God's plan for your life is peace. When everything is in a hopeless mess, remember that is not God's choice. ". . . my peace I give unto you. . ." Jesus said. "For I know the thoughts that I think toward you, saith the Lord, thoughts of peace, and not of evil, to give you an expected end" (John 14:27; Jeremiah 29:11).

Your Creator wants the interior of you to be peaceful, controlled, balanced, whole—free within itself. Although there will be confusion, frustration, suffering, and chaos on the exterior, Jesus gives you the freedom of peace for the interior—when you allow.

But you have to allow. You have to let Him be the leader. You have to give Him control.

Because we live in a world of natural law where tornadoes, colliding cars, terminal illnesses are facts . . .

Because we live in a world where other people have free choice . . . and those choices may affect our lives directly . . . bringing divorce, alienation, war, discrimination, injustice, and other unpleasant evils . . .

Because we live in a world where we have free choice and we are often not guided by God in our decisions . . . there will be flagrant mix-ups in our lives, acute suffering, even stark tragedy. . . .

Because these are truths, you need to understand that in spite of all the exterior confusion, that inner peace can remain undisturbed. *If* you allow. The freedom of that choice is in your hands.

You have to allow His peace to be yours. He will never intrude. But you have the freedom to ask Him to guide your life; and in that freedom, you will find the reality of His peace.

Let me tell you about Donna.

She was brilliant in English Literature. Her teachers told her that she would surely win the scholarship given by the local literary club.

No one could win over Donna.

She began a systematic study to prepare for the exam early in her senior year. Then she won the lead in the senior play.

Rehearsals of the play consumed most of her free time. Her English teacher expressed concern about the scholarship, but Donna breezily told her not to worry. She was confident she would win. No one had ever scored higher than Donna.

Her English teacher pleaded with her about priorities. She understood the play was great fun, but winning the scholarship meant full expenses for four years of college.

But Donna continued with the long hours spent on the play. She had always been the best. She was sure she would be again.

But she wasn't.

The exam was given the day following the final performance of the play. The day of the exam, Donna was physically and emotionally weary . . . and mentally unprepared for the difficulty of the questions. A slow, quiet girl who had persistently studied during the year won the scholarship.

Donna was devastated.

She came to our parsonage filled with self-hatred, remorse, and the assurance that her life was ruined. After her flood of weeping subsided, we went into the kitchen and sat at the table with hot cocoa and cookies.

There, we talked about the fact that even the most sincere of us make errors in judgment.

"How could I have been so stupid?" was her suffering question.

The answer: Because you are human. Because you haven't lived very long and you could hardly have attained a sophisticated degree of wisdom or maturity.

"But it was so wrong!" she would burst out.

And the tears would flood again.

"It was an honest mistake," I told her. "God knows that. Don't waste time and energy now piling foolish guilt on yourself.

"You made a mistake. Your life will never go as you had planned. But that does not, for a moment, mean that it will not go! The Creator God is a Redeemer God who will enable you to make creative use even of mistakes.

"He is not only a Redeemer of sin; He is a Redeemer of circumstance as well."

It was hard for her to believe. She wanted to punish herself. But that was useless.

I challenged Donna to open herself to what use God could make of the mistake. I reminded her that she would have found a way to go to college had there been no literary scholarship. She must now open herself so that God could creatively help her use the error in such a way that His plan could go on in her life.

"Focus on the Redeemer God," I pleaded. "Refuse to allow your mind to dwell on the shattered dream. Refuse to heap guilt on yourself for not being wiser."

She agreed to try. It was painfully difficult. Self-pity was such a temptation.

But, determinedly, she strove to keep her focus on the God who redeems situations . . . as well as sin . . . the God who does not turn away when we are humanly stupid.

During her first year of college, Donna worked in the dormitory kitchen to help pay expenses. Toward the end of that year, she was called to the dean's office. He told her that her superiors had been impressed with her ability to relate to the other members of the kitchen crew and had recommended her for a position on the student counseling services. She looked at the dean in astonishment.

Donna had heard of the elite group of students handpicked by the administration who were available for counseling with other students. It was easier for some persons to share confusions with a peer than with an administrator. It was both an honor and an opportunity for service to be a student counselor.

Donna was delighted.

And then came something she had not known: the position came with a full scholarship.

When she called me long-distance to shout the news of the Redeemer God at work in her life, we both laughed and cried. I remember her words clearly, "God didn't cause my stupidity; but He used it for good."

How true that was.

Donna would have done student counseling for free. Now it came, complete with scholarship. And she rejoiced. "The opportunity could have never been mine, in all probability, if I hadn't blown the other scholarship and had to work in the kitchen!"

Do you understand the lesson Donna learned?

God didn't make the judgmental error. But when Donna, with free choice, did, the Redeemer God used it in working "all things together for good to them that love God."

Here is how to handle "all that freedom!" Use it to focus on God.

Had Donna remained depressed and feeling defeated, I doubt she would ever have made an attempt to go to college. She would have been so busy making herself pay for the mistake that she could not be open to God's use of it.

It was only when Donna deliberately turned her mental focus from self-denigration to the loving Redeemer God that her spirits began to rise and she was able to find the courage to make application for college. She was able to swallow her pride and work at the menial chores of the kitchen instead of sitting leisurely back among the "scholarshipped elite."

By determinedly focusing on God, Donna was free to follow. He was free to redeem. And beautiful, creative use was made of Donna's judgmental error.

Give yourself to God's guidance.

That is how you can be the best liberated you!

How Can You Best Relate to Others?

Five

Brighten the Corner Where You Are

We cannot all be famous
or be listed in 'Who's Who,'
But every person great or small
has important work to do,
For seldom do we realize
the importance of small deeds
Or to what degree of greatness
unnoticed kindness leads—
For it's not the big celebrity
in a world of fame and praise,
But it's doing unpretentiously
in undistinguished ways
The work that God assigned to us,
unimportant as it seems,
That makes our task outstanding
and brings reality to dreams—
So do not sit and idly wish
for wider, new dimensions
Where you can put in practice
your many 'Good Intentions'—
But at the spot God placed you
begin at once to do
Little things to brighten up
the lives surrounding you,
For if everybody brightened up
the spot on which they're standing
By being more considerate
and a little less demanding,
This dark old world would very soon
eclipse the 'Evening Star'
If everybody *Brightened Up
the Corner Where They Are!*

HELEN STEINER RICE

How Can You Be Popular?

I

To be a girl ... Those words seem to snap a portrait in most people's minds of the cover girl of *Seventeen* who is gorgeous, articulate, exciting, talented, outgoing, and who has young males standing in line at her door.

To be a girl ... To be popular ... aren't those two states synonymous? Perhaps. In romantic fiction.

In real life, however, few of us even remotely resemble the cover girl of *Seventeen*. Some of us are quiet; some inarticulate. Some have no performing skills; some are reserved. Few have young males standing in line at their doors.

Does this mean that the extraordinary few are the only ones who have a chance at popularity?

I don't think so.

I think the answer depends on your definition of the term. So let's talk about it.

When I was in high school, Beverly Thomas was the closest person to a *Seventeen* cover girl we had. Dark hair, dark eyes, great figure, terrific clothes, talented in music and speech, talkative and outgoing, leadership charisma and great charm—and she was a band majorette! We all watched her every move and sighed about how wonderful she was!

Beverly was, by any standards, POPULAR.

Then there was Cynthia Whitefield. She was of average height, chubby, wore average clothes, was quiet, good in shorthand, steady, kind, gentle, and a loyal friend—and she rarely, if ever, dated. We paid little attention to Cynthia in our gossip sessions, but when we needed help with a tough assignment or a ride home or we just needed to feel comfortable with someone who cared, Cynthia seemed to be there.

Cynthia was, by few standards, POPULAR.

And yet, she was always a class officer; she was quietly beloved by faculty and students alike. So, although we didn't call her wonderful, she was popular.

The dictionary defines *popularity* as "commonly liked, approved, found praiseworthy." But there are two levels (at least) of that state.

There is POPULARITY.

There is popularity.

One is the scintillating-Beverly kind.

One is the steady-Cynthia kind.

Both are of equal value.

You have one or the other, depending on what is true for you. But one is never superior to the other. They are both vital in our world.

It is true that one is more flashy than the other. That does not make one of greater worth.

When Beverly sang the lead in the school operetta . . . When Beverly was crowned Football Queen . . . When Beverly came out at the Senior Banquet in her stunning, blue dress to sing the latest hit song . . . there was more glamour and sensational excitement . . . there was more chatter and discussion . . . there were more flashbulbs popping than when Cynthia quietly typed up programs for the school operetta . . . when Cynthia yelled as a member of the Pep Club . . . when Cynthia went to the Senior Banquet alone. Beverly was POPULAR. Cynthia was popular.

There was a difference. But only in kind. Not in value.

One is not superior to the other.

They are equal. And they both have responsibilities to others.

If you are POPULAR, you will be looked up to, emulated, respected . . . and that demands a lot from you. Such POPULARITY is not a free gift. It brings burdens with it. Because people pay tribute to you with their admiration, affection, respect, you have an obligation to return the tribute by always being your very best self.

Such POPULARITY will only be a moment-in-the-sun, a flash-in-the-pan, unless you are genuinely involved and concerned with others. This POPULARITY also brings pitfalls. Because others think you are wonderful, you may begin to believe yourself superior. And when you fall into that trap, you are headed straight for heartbreak. If it doesn't come in high school, it will probably come in the first days of college when you are on the same dormitory floor with twenty-four other girls voted "most popular" in high school.

On the other hand, if you are the popular type of personality, you, too, will be looked up to, emulated, respected—in a different way. But such admiration also makes demands. Such popularity is not a free gift. It, too, brings burdens with it. People pay tribute to you with their friendship, their confidence in you, their reliance on you. You have an obligation to return the tribute by always being your very best self. You have earned a special place in your group. You will have to be careful to be worthy of it.

Whether you are POPULAR or popular, you must open yourself to ways in which you may be of service to others. Consider Beverly and Cynthia. Both girls were involved in the entire school program. One in the spotlight. One behind the scenes. Both contributing to us all.

Both Beverly and Cynthia were *There you are!* kind of people. Each was concerned with giving of herself, in her own unique way, to others.

That is a mature characteristic. It comes hard to most of us. We are all born announcing *Here I am!* To move from that comfortable haven takes a lot of courage. Most of us are basically shy, and we take refuge in what is familiar to us. We are afraid to focus on someone else.

When I was fourteen, shyness kept me trapped in the *Here I am!* group. A POPULAR senior girl came into study hall, sat beside me, and tried to start a conversation. I remember opening my mouth, but I was so terrified that I could not make any words come out.

She finally assumed I must be a mute and turned her attention elsewhere.

Well, I'm very shy, I consoled myself as I buried my burning face in a book. *It's okay that I behaved like that because I am young and insecure.*

But as the blanket of self-pity covered me, I had a flash of perception that startled me. That kind of thinking was a blanket, a refuge from reality. It was a cop-out! Unless I made another decision, I would forever be a *Here I am!* person.

I decided I was going to have to change my focus from self to others. I was going to have to become a *There you are!* kind of person. At least I would try.

That night, there was a class party. I went with a girl friend who promised to try to help me focus on other people.

When we arrived, people were already going down the buffet line filling their plates. I was in a total panic. I knew I would not know one thing to say to anyone.

But the boy who was serving sloppy joes grinned at me. My friend who had promised to help nudged me hard.

Palms sweating, eyes glazed with agonized fright, my voice squeaked out, "Those really look great! How do you make them?"

"Hey! Thanks for noticing!" the boy boomed at me. "This is my own original recipe. I think I make the best sloppy joes in the world. I want to have a whole chain of sloppy-joe drive-ins someday."

Overcome with my success in actually talking to someone I didn't know, I wished him well with his future plans and moved on down the line. My heart was almost jumping out of my body. For two sentences, I had been a *There you are!* kind of person. I felt the warm glow of the gift I had given.

It was not a very splashy beginning. But it was a beginning. And that is how to move from the shyness of *Here I am!* to the givingness of *There you are!* It is really quite simple: You turn your attention to someone else.

You don't have to say a lot. The best conversationalists in the world are those who don't say much. That surprised me when I discovered it because I was certain that I would have to utter great knowledge with every breath. But that is not only unnecessary; it is not usually the greatest gift.

When I think about it, the people I enjoy talking with the most are those who want to listen to me. As I have explored it with others, I have found that to be a universal.

What all people yearn for—what everyone cherishes—is a person who is willing to listen. Anthony Quinn recently said that the quality he admired most in Aristotle Onassis was his ability to listen. Quinn told an interviewer, "There are three others on my 'Great Listeners' List: John Barrymore, Greta Garbo, Katherine Hepburn; Onassis was the fourth. He had the rare gift of making one's inanities sound important." What greater gift could one give another? Onassis and indeed all people willing to listen are *There you are!* kind of people.

So, if shyness has been cementing you in the *Here I am!* group, change your focus from yourself to other people. Even in something as simple as asking a boy how he makes sloppy joes. That was my beginning. It wasn't profound conversation, but it was directed at another person. And that transformed me from taker to giver. I, squeaking voice, sweating palms, and all, showed my interest in the boy before me. In effect, I was saying: *There you are!* and he responded with joy.

If this is a problem to you, make a decision to open yourself to others just as you are. Involve yourself with others in whatever ways are true and honest to you. Be supportive of others as they attempt to live the ways that are true and honest to them.

When Beverly (or whatever is the name of the superstar in your group) sings a terrific song, be in the audience cheering like crazy. That is your contribution to the social event. It is a valuable one.

And when you meet your Beverly, instead of dropping your eyes and rushing by, go to her and say, "You were wonderful!"

She will respond with the same happiness that the boy with his special sloppy-joe recipe did! You are showing an interest in her; that makes you special to her immediately. Your compliment is a gift, and she will receive it with a warm glow.

And you will go on down the hall with a warm glow because you will have just moved from *Here I am!* to *There you are!* You gave your attention to another! You gave the gift of caring about someone else.

And when you do that, I guarantee that popularity can be yours.

But such popularity also brings pitfalls.

One of these is that because others do not swarm around you as they gather around the POPULAR personality, you may begin to believe yourself inferior. If you fall into that trap, you are headed for heartbreak. It is a lie that distorts all that is true and honest for you. It can erode all the splendid attributes that are yours. It can snatch from those in your world the unique gifts that only you can give.

Accept the value of your God-created self and you will be relieved of the severe (and completely unnecessary) pain that so many youths (and adults for that matter) daily suffer because they are not the dazzling personalities that are POPULAR. God created you as you are because He had a dream for you. You have value. As you are.

Author and news correspondent Brenda Ueland has said that the key to successful living with others is "walk, be alone, and talk to the Lord you know. Find out about yourself, look inward and outward both. You have to find your center and live from that."

How can you be popular?

First, move from the *Here I am!* group to the *There you are!* group.

Second, discover what level of popularity is true and honest for the uniqueness of you.

Third, walk with dignity on that level and develop every capacity for focusing on and giving to others that you can.

Fourth, thank God for the who of you He created and know every moment your unique value to yourself, your God, your family, your community, your world.

There has never been anyone on earth just like you. There is not now. There never will be again.

Wrapped in the knowledge of your special God-creation, you are free to focus on others. When you do, you will be respected, valued by all to whom you give your gift of caring. You will be popular.

How Can You Rid Yourself of Jealousy?

2

The temptation to be jealous often occurs as a result of the yearning to be popular. Webster defines *jealousy* as "apprehension," but that is rather a weak word for the way you may be tempted to feel toward the redhead who was just elected captain of the girls' basketball team two votes ahead of you or for the new blonde who just walked off with "your guy!"

Psychologists tell us that jealousy is a symptom of a lack of self-confidence and emotional security. What that really means is that you long so much for popularity and acceptance that it is hard for you to admit that those about you long for those same things—and often get them.

Jealousy is one of the most dangerous of all emotional hazards. It is like quicksand. Once you let yourself get involved in it, it is hard to pull out. You feel better to go into an emotional storm than to calmly watch your current male interest walk off to the pizza parlor with the new girl in town.

But it isn't better.

Jealousy undermines your confidence, your happiness, your security. Jealousy corrodes your inner balance.

Are you jealous? How would you react to the following situations?

1. When Gail was chosen to represent the school at a district leadership conference, did you make excuses for yourself? Did you say something such as, "Too bad that you don't have a chance in this school unless you are a sister of the star football player!" That is jealousy.

2. When the girls are in a huddle and someone comments that Shary is a doll, do you hurriedly add a "Yes, but if I had the clothes she does . . ." comment? Does it annoy you to hear Shary complimented? Whenever you feel an urge to follow a compliment with a "yes, but . . ." sentence, you are probably jealous.

3. Do you spend too much time running over in your mind the attributes of one girl? Do you spend time going over the many reasons you dislike her? Do you enjoy saying piously, "I think it is too bad that Ann always runs after boys the way she does. She would be cute if she weren't such a chaser!" Analyze that closely. The problem may not be Ann. It may be that you are jealous.

4. When the special boy in your life takes out another girl, is your reaction frustration and pain? If so, consider it carefully. Is your torment caused from a real feeling for this one boy? Very often, it will be rooted in jealousy.

Jealousy destroys. It brings harm to you and to those about you. And it is a ridiculous waste of time and energy.

While you are lying across the bed thinking about the reasons you dislike Shary with the pretty clothes, you are wasting the time you could be spending cutting and sewing a new dress for yourself.

While you are in the "harpy huddle" criticizing Ann for her popularity with men, you could be working on the inner poise that allows you to focus on another which is so attractive in Ann. The male species do not "go" for a girl who is jealous! Jealousy embarrasses them and is one of the quickest ways to dissolve a relationship. And it is easily spotted in your conversation.

Someone will say, "I heard that Rhonda was chosen Queen of the County Fair." And you say, "Sure, if my father were president of the bank, I would be too!" Your listeners know you're jealous!

If Laura gives a wonderful monologue at a party, everyone may crowd about her with congratulations and praise. If you stand on the sidelines and say, "Oh, haven't you heard that thing before? I have just dozens of times!" You haven't hurt Laura. You have hurt yourself in the view of others for they will know that you're jealous.

Remember my high school list where I actually wrote down my yearning to be like Shary in clothes, like Margaret in piano, like Edna Rhe in humor? I wanted to be like those girls because I did not know *who* Ruth was. I did not know Ruth's unique value.

And in the lack of that self-knowledge, jealousy sprouts its ugly head.

In the hypothetical examples given here, you can see the problem clearly. You want to be Queen of the County Fair like Rhonda. You want to be a good monologist like Laura. You want to be popular like Ann. You want to have great clothes like Shary.

But God created you beautifully unique. One-of-a-kind. Never-before-on-earth. Never-to-be-again. There is no one like you. You will never be like anyone else.

This is what you must learn. And when you do, you can draw all your attention to the distinctive God-created strengths that are yours. You have no need to be *like* another.

And in that understanding, you can face reality and be at peace with it. You can know some joys will never be yours. But you will know that God will give you other joys. You look at what is true for you, and you can rid yourself of jealousy.

Think back to the hypothetical examples used here.

Since physical beauty is usually a prime requisite, it may be that you are so structured that you will never be Queen of the County Fair. That is a fact you may have to accept. That accolade may be true for Rhonda; it may not be true for you.

Because giving a good monologue requires a dynamic flair, a sense of timing for comedy punch lines, and dramatic skills, it may be that you will never give a sensational monologue at a party. That may be your personal fact. What is true for Laura is not true for you.

Because POPULARITY requires a specially magnetic personality, it may be that you will never know those kinds of skyrockets. That could be a fact that is yours. It is true for the uniqueness of you.

Because the most up-to-date wardrobe costs a great deal of money, your family's financial status may prohibit your having a shot at being "best dressed" in the high school annual. That is a fact in your life.

But although these may be facts, they are not bad facts. Nor are they defeating facts. They are merely that—facts.

You don't have to be afraid of them. You need never feel threatened by another's success if you keep your confidence in God's creation of the very special you.

If something is not true to you, accept the fact without bitterness. Rejoice that there are beautiful, dramatically talented, high-fashion women who add sparkle to your world. But also rejoice for you. Their gifts make your world a brighter place because of who they are.

Most important rejoice that you were also created to contribute something. Your contributions to the world may be different but they are just as vital, just as important, as theirs.

If beauty, dramatic talent, high fashion are true to you, but there has been no opportunity for their development yet, you can be assured that God will guide your life until those doors open and you find ways of using these talents for Him.

Whatever is true to you will become reality if you stay close to God and allow Him to lead. He created you, and He is not the author of frustration. He does not give gifts to plague you for denied fulfillment. He gives gifts that, in His workings in your life, will find fulfillment. In His way. In His time. If you trust Him.

Let me tell you about my sister-in-law, Margaret.

She has been, since childhood, an exceptional pianist and one of the great loves of her life has been chic clothes. When she was fifteen, she felt a God-call to be a missionary. With her limited understanding of missions, she thought that to accept this call would mean that her piano-playing days were over. Who ever heard of pianos in the primitive jungles and mud huts where missionaries live? The only pictures of missionaries she had seen were of people in drab, dismal clothes with hair tied back in a knot at the neck. So her love for fashion would have to be abandoned.

Even with that painful perception, Margaret told God she would be a missionary for Him. She went to college, married my red-haired brother preparing for missionary service, and made application for her church to send her where they would.

And they did. To the Cape Verde Islands.

She did not live in a mud hut. She lived in a nice house where she had a piano on which she could play and give music lessons. She had an organ in her church which she played for services. She directed a large choir of singers. She played the piano on a radio show broadcast throughout the Islands. Her musical skills were in constant use.

And clothes?

Her major assignment was in the Bible College, where she trained young ministers and their wives. She dressed as attractively as possible for this leadership role. Prior to leaving America, she was asked to take a wardrobe of formal wear because she would be invited to state functions. Because Cape Verde, at that time, was a Portuguese possession, the dictator of Portugal visited the Islands, and I have a photograph of Margaret, in beautiful formal fashion, greeting this world leader.

The things that were true to Margaret became realities. In God's way. In God's time. When you understand what is true for you, jealousy becomes an irrelevant emotion. You cannot be all things, but what is God-created true for you will be your gift to the world and will bring you personal fulfillment.

Earlier in this book, I told you about Valerie, a girl who ran out of my speech class crying. The reason for her tears, you may remember, was that public speaking brought joy to her older sister, but it terrified Valerie. It was untrue to Valerie and brought only frustration and pain.

When she gained that self-knowledge, how stupid it would be for her to ever be jealous of the glamour of her sister's professional television career. Valerie found her own career that brought personal satisfaction. She did not need to be like her sister. She has only to be true to the value of herself. Then she can rejoice in her sister's joy—and in her own. Thus she is released from jealousy.

Long ago, I came across this prayer written by Thomas a Kempis. I penned it on the flyleaf of my Bible. Since then, I have spent hundreds of hours attempting to pray it honestly. The words are easy enough to read. They are difficult to mean.

O Lord, Thou knowest what is the better way:
Let this or that be done as Thou shalt please.
Give what Thou wilt, and how much Thou wilt, and when Thou wilt.
Deal with me as Thou knowest, and best pleaseth Thee,
And is most for Thy honor.
Set me where Thou wilt, and deal with me in all things as Thou wilt.
I am in Thy hands; turn me round and turn me back again, even as a
   wheel.
Behold I am Thy servant, prepared for all things.
For I desire not to live unto myself, but unto Thee;
And oh! That I could do it worthy and perfectly!

When you can pray that prayer and mean it, you will have the kind of trust in your Creator-God that will free you from jealousy. For here you are affirming that He will give what is true to you. In His way. In His time. You need not be in a strain. He has promised.

What is true for you will come to you. If it is untrue to you, you would be unhappy with it.

So you can be at peace ... when Rhonda is crowned Queen; when Laura gives a great monologue; when Ann is POPULAR; when Shary dresses like a fashion ad in *Seventeen.* Their achievements are no threat to you because you and God are working together to develop what is true to the beautiful uniqueness of you.

There can be no one like you! You are one-of-a-kind special!

How Can You Handle the Problem of Pride?

3

Webster defines *pride* as being anything from a state of satisfaction taken in something accomplished to a high opinion of one's own importance, merit, or superiority. The accompanying synonyms for pride are haughtiness, vainglory, egotism.

We usually think of pride in regard to one's estimate of personal superiority. This can be a real problem to the POPULAR personality. When everyone adores you, it is easy for you to adore you, too—and that will set you up for a tremendous fall. Adoration always involves superiority and inferiority.

When I was young, there was a minister's wife whom I adored! I thought she was perfection in every way.

When I would express my adoration to her, I could sense her discomfort. I wondered why because I knew I would be delighted if someone adored me. But one day, it dawned on me that such an attitude was unhealthy. Both for her and for me. Adoration always divides into superiority and inferiority. She knew that if she agreed with my adoration, she would be in for a fall when she confronted her faults and weaknesses. I understood that for me to set someone else on a pedestal placed me in an inferior position and that was wrong for the God-created me.

I had freely used the verb *adore* until that sudden insight. Since then, I have deleted it from my vocabulary. Not because I don't have supreme respect and admiration for many people, but because I do not place their value above my own. I recognize that they, too, have weaknesses; I recognize that I, too, have strengths. We both have value.

The term *adoration* can lead into a trap. There is always the temptation for a magnetically gifted person to feel superiority when others "adore" him or her. There is also the temptation for those with gifts less scintillating to feel inferiority when they "adore" those who sparkle. It's a vicious trap and should be avoided.

Thomas Jefferson wrote long ago, you remember, "[We] are created equal!" In God's Creator-view, one is never of more importance than another. Understand that; believe it; make it a part of your daily creed of living.

When I was a college professor, the problem of pride kept cropping up in counseling sessions. Finally, I decided it should be dealt with in depth. I invited a group of girls who were fighting with this to my house for a slumber party. My family was out of town and so these girls brought their pajamas and came for a whole night of fun with a professor!

Late in the evening, we got into pajamas, sat around a roaring fire with a huge bowl of buttered popcorn, and began to talk about this thorny issue of pride. We agreed it was insidious. It creeps in without our knowing or understanding. Often it is unclear whether the root is inferiority or superiority.

I, who usually have a pad and pencil with me, kept notes on the discussion. Let me share with you some of the stories.

Gigi

The first girl to speak was Gigi. She was one of the POPULAR girls. She never entered a room without its taking on a brighter glow.

Gigi told us of the time when she was invited by the handsome captain of the track team to be his date at the Senior Luncheon. As an underclassman, she felt honored to be allowed to go. Her girl friends shared her joy.

But when her mother told her there would be no money for a new dress, she was swamped with feelings that she should stay home. Every girl there would have on a new dress, said Gigi's pride. It would be better to turn the date down than to go and be embarrassed by not having a new dress. Her newest dress had been worn twice, and everyone was surely sick of it by now!

Pride caused a big furor the day of the luncheon. Instead of happy hours of preparation and anticipation, Gigi could only sob because she had no new dress to wear.

Then the florist rang the doorbell and her sister ran up the stairs screaming, "He sent you an orchid!" But Gigi only looked at it dolefully. She couldn't enjoy the delight of her first orchid!

At the luncheon Gigi discovered that many girls did not have new dresses. Only then did she remember that she had worn her white dress only to a family reunion and an afternoon music recital. Probably no one at the luncheon was present at either occasion.

But, even if they were, she was now beginning to understand that the newness of the dress was not the important thing. What was important was Gigi, the girl inside.

Polly

Nibbling popcorn around a roaring fire, the next person to share was a quiet little girl, Polly, who worked in the college kitchen. She was sitting by the POPULAR Gigi, and I noticed Gigi holding her hand, urging her to share and be a part of the group.

Polly and Gigi had been in high school together. One weekend, Polly's brother who was in college had invited her to come up for a weekend. When Gigi heard the news, she had offered to let Polly wear her new black coat.

Polly refused. She felt it was an insult to her pride.

"But it wasn't," the irresistible Gigi pointed out. "I only wanted her to have the grandest time and I had a new black coat that would just be perfect!"

"I know," Polly admitted ruefully. "Gigi was being my friend."

"And pride should never have opened its nasty little mouth," asserted Gigi. "All human relations are based on sharing. Pride cheated Polly out of the fun of wearing my black coat on her big, college weekend. It was too high a price."

"But would you have accepted a dress from someone to wear to the luncheon?" asked a girl across the popcorn bowl.

Gigi grinned. "Great question! I probably wouldn't have. And I would have been as wrong as Polly. Boy! Pride is really an expensive item, isn't it?"

And we all agreed.

Rebecca

"I didn't get to go to the Senior Prom," Rebecca told us, "because I didn't receive an invitation until Friday morning and the prom was that night.

"If I accepted the date, I felt that Jerry would know that he had saved me from going stag, he would know that I hadn't had any other invitations."

Because of pride Rebecca stayed home, missing the excitement of the prom and never having a chance to know what a great date Jerry might have been. Rebecca admitted that pride was little comfort to her as she sat at home, knowing her friends were enjoying themselves at the prom.

Rebecca also admitted she never pondered the reason that Jerry had waited to call her until the morning of the prom.

"Could it be," I asked her, "that he had to wait that long to be sure he had enough money for a corsage, gas in the car, and Cokes after? It may never have occurred to him that you would go into a huff because he did not call you earlier."

Rebecca nodded. "I know. He worked at a service station for all his spending money. I think you're probably right. But my pride told me he had to call earlier. I was wrong."

Shelly

"I guess expectation of how we want a male to treat us is one of our biggest problems," Shelly commented. "I really learned that the hard way."

Shelly explained that the football hero of her school, David, had asked her out for dinner. She pictured an evening of stars, romance, and poetry.

She and David entered the restaurant. After they had ordered, Shelly said, David began a long harangue about football plays which she understood as clearly as an advanced course in Greek.

"I'll bet," Gigi said, "he never once mentioned your beauty. Stars, romance didn't come up. Certainly he didn't even approach poetry!"

"No," Shelly grinned, "but he did deliver an eloquent discourse on the 'wishbone offense,' whatever that is. But pride told me that, football hero or not, I couldn't be treated that way. I wanted dates my way. So that was the end of David in my life. Pride would keep me company, of course, and my pride wouldn't discuss football.

"I realize now," Shelly concluded, "that if David hadn't admired me, he wouldn't have asked me to dinner. His whole world revolved around football and he wanted to share it. My preset conditions that he emulate Robert Redford were dumb. But I didn't know it then."

Emily

"I lost a boy because of pride," said Emily. "We had a date for church. Two minutes before Jack was supposed to arrive, he called and said he couldn't make it. I went with my parents. He came to my locker the next morning to explain, but I refused to speak to him. My pride had been damaged. I expected him to beg for forgiveness. He didn't bother. Instead, he took Caryl to church the next time. He never asked me out again.

"I found out later that the reason Jack called at the last minute to tell me he couldn't take me to church was because his father's car had broken down and he had no way to come for me. He wasn't deliberately mistreating me. He expected me to understand. I wanted him to grovel. I was wrong!" Emily said.

Before we finished for the evening, I shared with the group a time during my own high school years when pride threw me into a tizzy.

Ruth

The first time I invited my high school group to my parsonage home, pride almost did me in.

I looked at my home and compared it to those of some of my friends. I begged my mother to buy a new tablecloth. The old one had a scorch in the center. Many of my friends had spinet pianos. I was ashamed of the old upright in the living room.

I wrung my hands, paced the floor, and shed tears of fearful anxiety. Why? Because pride made me distort reality.

I understand that now. But then pride had ruined my glow of anticipation.

My mother baked two chocolate cakes and three batches of cookies. She made a large bowl of punch. With all that on the table, who could possibly see the scorched spot in the center?

Equally absurd was my concern over the old upright. It had a good tune and with one of us playing and a dozen teenagers draped about it focusing on "beautiful harmony," do you think anyone noticed that the piano wasn't brand-new?

Of course not!

I had gone into a whirlwind of anxiety because I had allowed pride to make me forget that value never lies in things. Value lies in people, in happiness, in sharing, in good times, in the warm acceptance of my home.

After I had ended my story, I looked about at the girls sharing in the warm unity of this moment. I felt the insights we had shared would help them handle the problem of pride in the future.

How can *you* handle the problem of pride?

We all agreed that night that the only time when pride should enter our life is when we can use the word "self-respect" or "dignity" in place of the word "pride." Self-respect will cause you to keep your hair well-groomed, your clothes mended, your lessons up-to-date. Self-respect will cause you to be thorough in your research for your term paper, keep your room clean, your shoes polished. Self-respect will keep you from cheating on exams, complaining about your family, being loud at parties. Self-respect will make you refrain from trying to tag along with a group when you haven't been invited, giggling at off-color jokes, arguing in public.

What you've already accomplished in your life gives you a sense of dignity that goes under the heading of "pride." This type of pride, however, lets you focus on the unique worth of the God-created you.

You are neither superior nor inferior. You are friends with all—open in understanding of human problems and weaknesses—ever eager to share.

You have dignity. When you understand that, you have the answer to how to handle the problem of pride.

How Can You Control Your Anger?

4

Have you ever stopped to estimate how much time and energy you have wasted on things not worth the price? In the last chapter we explored some expenses of pride. But what about anger? Or, in more extreme moments, utter fury!

This is an emotion that demands much from us, damages many precious parts of our lives, and is often destructive—even in small things.

There is the belt that won't stay fastened. There is the closet door that won't stay shut. There is the button on your new green blouse that keeps popping off. These, and countless other little things, make you madder and madder until your patience snaps and fireworks explode.

And anger is always a waste. Always useless. Often irreparably harmful.

I have in my counseling notes an excellent example of anger on the warpath. I called my former student and asked if she minded if I used it in this book. She laughed and said, "Please do! It's taken me years to really begin to conquer anger and if I can help someone else with this emotion that has brought me so much pain, I want to."

Her name is Linda and she told me of one time when anger "did her in!" It was the night of the school-choir hayride. She had a new western outfit. As the school bell rang, her boyfriend, Ron, hurried by to remind her he would pick her up at seven. Sounded grand.

As she tossed her books into the locker, a friend, Gary, came by and asked her to run over a piece of music with him. He had his trumpet so it would only take a few minutes.

Two hours later, she hurried home.

Hastily, she drew her bath water and took out the western outfit. After her bath, she went to the dresser. She couldn't find her comb. The drawer stuck. It always did when she was in a hurry.

After a few yanks, she jerked with all her force and out flew the drawer, emptying its contents on the floor. She began to grab bottles, rollers, brushes, and combs. As she wildly scrambled for the rolling, tumbling objects, her little sister ran in whirling a lariat over her head. It was the one that came on Linda's new western outfit purchased especially for the hayride!

Now unwound, Linda knew she would never be able to get it back on the loops in the "cowboy manner" it had been.

"Judy, give me that lariat and you get out of here right this minute."

Wide-eyed, Judy handed her the lariat. Her mother came in and took stock of the situation.

To Linda, she said, "I told you yesterday to sew that lariat in place; it was bound to slip off. It was not put on for any permanence."

Her mother went over to see if she could repair the lariat as Linda's voice rose to a shriek, "Mother! If all you know how to do is lecture, just leave me alone! Can't you see I'm late and now you want to yell at me! Just leave it alone and I'll fix it! I didn't ask for your help anyway!"

From the big armchair in the living room, over the clamor of the television, came a deep booming voice: the voice of authority. Linda's father.

"If you can't speak to your sister and your mother in a nicer way than that, I don't believe you should be allowed out among other people. Until you learn to control yourself, you can stay at home."

The end.

When Linda and I were discussing her problem with anger in my office, she told me this example. We analyzed it together. What caused it all?

First, Gary made her late. Her comb was misplaced. The drawer stuck. That set the stage. But her anger exploded over an imitation lariat!

An imitation lariat caused Linda to waste all that time, energy, and emotion. Ultimately, it caused her to miss a fun-packed hayride with the guy she liked best.

It was the most expensive price she had paid for anger. She had to break a date and stay at home in tears while Ron had to go on the hayride alone and be bored.

Anger had always been a problem for Linda. But until that evening it had never seemed so destructive.

There was the curler that came off during the night before cheerleader tryouts. She stomped it into the floor. But, she could buy another one at the dime store.

Banging the door to her room often knocked the facing loose, but it wasn't a major repair.

Breaking a record that stuck in the middle was no big deal, but it made her "feel better" to vent her anger on the "old thing!"

Stomping the stray curler, banging the door, breaking the record were release valves, Linda had rationalized. She had seen nothing wrong with anger until the night of the hayride. Then she began to understand that, by allowing herself to blow up over those minor things, she had formed a habit pattern that proved disastrous later on. Not only the missed date, but she understood that she had set up a reaction to life that, if continued, could become more and more destructive.

Sitting in my office, she quoted an old cliché she had not understood before. Now she did. It was: "For my own sake, I cannot afford to be angry."

"How can I control my anger?" she asked me. "It has seemed to just be a part of my nature. I have a high-strung personality. My mother is cool, calm, collected. It is her temperament. Mine is excitable and nervous. Is that the difference?"

Perhaps.

Some personalities are certainly more tempted to give in to angry outbursts than others. But even if temperament is an explanation, how does that help? The problem still exists. And for some people, like Linda, it can be crucial.

I know a person well who, literally, lives alone. Alone in a way that is difficult to imagine. No one visits her. Few write to her. Few call her.

When I call occasionally, long-distance, I am immediately in for a monologue on her ill treatment. I sympathize with her. I also sympathize with her family and friends who have, one by one, decided they can no longer tolerate her uncontrollable bursts of anger.

Through the years, she gradually has been left completely alone. All because she never learned self-control, self-discipline, self-poise.

Hers is an extreme case, I admit. But it spotlights the truth of the destructiveness of uncontrolled anger. That is why I was so deeply concerned with Linda's problem when she brought it to me.

"Maybe that's just the way I am," Linda broke into my thoughts. "I mean, it just really seems that I can't help it! I just get so mad!"

"That may be true," I admitted slowly. "You may not be able to help it after these years of giving in to anger whenever you felt like it. But there is Someone who can help you help it!"

She grinned. She knew where we were headed. "You really think religion has anything to do with anger?"

I returned her grin. "I believe 'religion,' as you call it, has to do with everything!" And so I explained.

When we are "born again," we become members of the family of God. Although we have our same personal characteristics inherited from or environmentally inspired by our human families, we now have available to us a new inheritance. We are "born, not of blood, nor of the will of the flesh, nor of the will of man, but of God" (John 1:13).

God is your Creator. He knows "just the way" you are. He understands that and He will work with you according to the way He created you. But, He gave you the free will of choosing the habit patterns that dominate your life. It is your choice as to whether or not you allow Christ to act through you.

If that is your choice, you must also realize that forming habits takes time and so does re-forming them. If you have a pattern of reacting in anger to any frustration, allow yourself time to revamp that ingrained response.

It is easy to become filled with guilt or overwhelmed with a sense of failure if you don't have total control instantly after asking for God's help. I have seen so much useless agony spent on this one point.

You are not immediately "re-strung" when you open yourself to God's help. Because God so fiercely protects free will, He will rarely wave a magic wand over ingrained habit patterns. He will work with you and give His strength, wisdom, and courage. But to break old habits and replace them with new ones is usually a process that takes time, patience, persistence—with God there to help. God never overpowers us with His might. He gave the gift of choice. He respects it. It is always your choice.

When Christ is your center, He will give His power, His peace, His strength. That does not mean that you will never feel strained nerves again when the dresser drawer flies out, emptying its contents, and your little sister wafts your new imitation lariat aloft! That does not mean that you will never feel like screaming, "Not another lecture now!" That does not mean that you will never feel anger flush over you when you are under some kind of pressure.

What it means is that God will help you restructure your habit patterns, now uncontrolled, so that you will not "take out" the strained nerves, the frustration, the anger on everyone around and, in the process, unbalance your own emotional system.

What it means is that He is a Redeemer God who will be with you in the bad times and enable you to use, even the tendency toward anger, for learning to rely more on Him.

What it means is that you can ask Him to work with you in, moment by moment, day by day, controlling your anger until the habit patterns are restructured into those of acceptance and peace, even under strain. What it means is that if you ask Him to help He will.

How Can You Cope With Worry?

You sat up late last night worrying over a problem, a problem that was not real—except in your imagination.

Is that sentence a description of you? Occasionally? Maybe often?

In that secret part of your mind called reason, you understand that the problem isn't real, or at the most is unlikely, but still you cannot make the worry about it go away.

If this sounds familiar, it is because worry is almost a universal with our gender. Most women whom I know and of whom I read admit having spent loads of energy and hours of time worrying over troubles that simply did not exist.

From my observation of the boys and men I know, most males are not like this. Only we women. And boys and men cannot understand why we punish ourselves like this.

Some of it may be explained by the "feminine mystique." But I think there are some fundamental reasons why girls go through these times of fears, tears, and nail biting.

A lot of worry stems from a lack of experience in the world. When we try new things, we yearn for perfection and are afraid we won't be adequate. We also worry over physical problems and limitations. And, when something wonderful does happen to us, we worry that life can't be that great, there has to be some gimmick somewhere.

Since I have always been a prime example of a person with this problem, I will share out of my own life. There are so many "torture-times" that it is hard to choose.

Worry from lack of experience

When I was sixteen, I was asked to be a candlelighter in my cousin Sue's wedding. I had a soft blue dress with matching shoes.

I pictured myself coming down the aisle stately and slowly. I would climb the steps and begin lighting the candles.

Then, as I planned for the moment, a cold tingle went down my spine. I worried and fretted. What if my hand shook so much that the candle went out? What if, when I stretched to reach the top candle, I slipped off the step?

My mother was to play the piano for the wedding. What if her music fell off the piano? What if some of the notes on the instrument stuck? What if her mind went completely blank?

But my mother spent no time worrying about imaginary disasters. Why did she not feel anxious? And why did I?

My mother had played for dozens of weddings. She knew what problems were real and what problems were imaginary. And she knew how to deal with them.

Even if the music fell off the piano, even if the keys stuck, or even if her mind went blank, my mother knew that there would be a way through.

There always is, and life just keeps turning.

This was my first big wedding. My insecurity and fears stemmed from lack of experience. I was not accustomed to being in front of the large number of people who would be in attendance. I wanted to do well—and so I worried.

I was terrified that my hand would shake until the candle used to light the many candles would go out. But Sue told me that there were matches taped to the candlelabra. I could simply take one of them and relight my candle. That wouldn't be so terrible.

I worried that when I reached to light the top candle, I might slip off the step. If that happened, Sue explained, I should simply hold onto my poise, step back up, and finish lighting the candles. How bad would that be?

That is the first answer I would give you in coping with worry. Know that the longer you live, the less worry will hound you. Unless you specifically cling to it (as some women do), you will develop a calmness in facing all of life, even the unknown. You will have coped with so many situations that confidence becomes a part of the *who* of you. The more you experience living, the more confidence you will have in your ability to handle whatever situations arise.

Worry over physical problems

When I was seventeen and a senior in high school, my brother wrote from college that he had a date lined up for me and wanted me to come to the campus. We would double-date for the homecoming game. How exciting!

I raced to the closet to check on what I would absolutely have to have in new clothes—and then I stopped. Oh! What if I had another bout with acne such as I had had the month before? It was terrible! Maybe I'd better stay home. I buried my face in an old blouse in the closet and sobbed.

I went to that college weekend with much trepidation. The terrible case of acne I worried about didn't develop. But I saw that weekend that there were many people on that college campus with acne. Everyone has it at some time or another. Had it happened to me, I could have handled it with poise and few, if anyone, would have even noticed it.

Years later, as an adult, I was scheduled to be a speaker for a national women's retreat. The day before leaving, I developed a huge, red boil on the end of my nose! The doctor said nothing could be done until it was ready to be lanced. He put a Band-Aid on my nose, and the next day I took a plane to the retreat.

Once there, I became so caught up in meeting the women, sharing with them, laughing and crying with them, that I actually forgot about my bandaged, swollen nose. And I doubt that many in attendance paid much attention to it.

That is the second answer I would give you in coping with worry. Minor physical problems come to us all. The way to deal with them is simply to accept them as part of being human. Do what can be done to alleviate any problem there might be, then forget it and go on with life. If handled with poise, everyone else will forget it, too.

Worry that life can't be that wonderful

When I was eighteen and a freshman in college, I began dating a boy named Bill. I thought he was the most wonderful guy in the world.

A popular song that year was "You! You! You! I'm in love with you! You! You!"

I changed the lyrics and sang at the top of my voice, "Bill! Bill! Bill! I'm in love with Bill! Bill! Bill! Oh, it gives me such a thrill, when you say you love me, Bill!"

My friends and I giggled with the joy of it all.

But the bliss of all that excitement was shattered one night, and I came home early, lay on my bed, and cried.

Why? Because I was worried.

I had been in a talent show. Cheryl sang a solo; Janie played the piano; I gave a humorous monologue. Bill was in the audience applauding.

When I finished my monologue, I slipped out the backstage door and went to the dorm to lie in the darkness and cry. Why?

It seemed so logical to me then. I knew that Bill had dated both Cheryl and Janie before he met me. What if my performance hadn't been equal to theirs? Perhaps Bill would wish he weren't going with me after all. What if he wanted to break up? Maybe I had better do it tomorrow before he had the chance!

It was torment. I was in agony that night, in spite of the fact that Bill had been spending all of his free time with me—of his own free will—and he saw and chatted with Cheryl and Janie every day in classes.

The day after the talent show, Bill listened to all my fears, wiped away all my tears, and told me it was Ruth he loved. I remember sitting beside him studying his face intently, wondering if I dared to believe.

What if Bill had thought Cheryl and Janie performed "better" than I in the talent show? That didn't mean he had changed his mind about spending a lot of time with me. He wasn't dating me because of the way I could give a monologue or make an audience laugh. Bill was not dating the talent; Bill was dating the girl. And when I got to that point, the whole worry broke into ridiculous pieces and I understood how silly I had been.

Although there are many disappointments in life, it is also a fact that there are many glowing, radiant dreams-come-true. The American author, H. L. Mencken wrote, "Women are the supreme realists of the race." As realists, we are cautious about claiming joy, wonder, beauty— all the good things—when we know that in so many lives these do not exist.

Because Bill gave me such happiness, I thought, *Life just isn't that wonderful. There has to be a gimmick somewhere.* I was aware of the stresses and strains, the ups and downs of human relations. When I found myself in a daze of joy with Bill, I began to look for trouble. I didn't yet understand that, although bleak unhappiness is a part of life, so are splendid, wonderful things.

Begin to accept this third truth. The earlier you believe it, the less tears you will have to shed in "looking for the gimmick" that may not be there.

How can you cope with worry? Most of my answers for you are for the future. You have to grow into them:

• Know that the more you experience living the more confidence you will have in your ability to handle whatever situations arise.
• Accept physical problems as a part of being human.
• Understand that dreams can come true in lavish dimension.

But there is one more way to cope with worry that you can take and use now. You have to earn experience in living. But at this very moment, you can *get busy*. When you feel a case of anxiety coming on, get busy. In a whirl of activity, the seedling fears have no time to grow.

In The Living Bible, Philippians 4:6,7 reads: "Don't worry about anything; instead, pray about everything; tell God your needs and don't forget to thank him for his answers. If you do this, you will experience God's peace, which is far more wonderful than the human mind can understand. His peace will keep your thoughts and your hearts quiet and at rest as you trust in Christ Jesus."

How can you cope with worry? There is the ultimate answer.

How Can You Be a Beautiful Woman in Your World?

Six

A Tribute to All Daughters

Every home should have a daughter,
    for there's nothing like a girl
To keep the world around her
    in one continuous whirl . . .
From the moment she arrives on earth,
    and on through womanhood,
A daughter is a *female*
    who is seldom understood . . .
One minute she is laughing,
    the next she starts to cry,
Man just can't understand her
    and there's just no use to try . . .
She is soft and sweet and cuddly,
    but she's also wise and smart,
She's a wondrous combination
    of a mind and brain and heart . . .
And even in her baby days
    she's just a born coquette,
And anything she really wants
    she manages to get . . .
For even at a tender age
    she uses all her wiles
And she can melt the hardest heart
    with the sunshine of her smiles . . .
She starts out as a rosebud
    with her beauty unrevealed
Then through a happy childhood
    her petals are unsealed . . .
She's soon a sweet girl graduate,
    and then a blushing bride,
And then a lovely woman
    as the rosebud opens wide . . .
And some day in the future,
    if it be God's precious will,
She, too, will be a Mother
    and know that reverent thrill
That comes to every Mother
    whose heart is filled with love
When she beholds the "angel"
    that God sent her from above . . .
And there would be no life at all
    in this world or the other
Without a *darling daughter*
    who, in turn, becomes a *mother!*

HELEN STEINER RICE

How Can You Be Open to Others With No Prejudice?

Prejudice is prejudging without all the facts being in. Prejudice is looking at only one perspective. Prejudice is exclusion. Prejudice is immaturity.

I first became aware of prejudice when my father discovered that the black people in our Texas town did not have a church. Immediately, he, a white minister, began arrangements with the owner of the black community saloon for its use. Are you beginning to get a glimpse of the kind of man my father was?

The saloon was the largest building available in the community. So, just as he was unprejudiced in wanting to minister to *all* people regardless of color, so was he unprejudiced about *where* he did the ministering!

On Thursday night and Sunday afternoon, my father would go to the saloon where he and the bartender hung a sheet over the liquor cabinet so thoughts could turn to God! They would arrange the chairs and tables so that entire families could sit together. Then my father would stand beneath the blinking neon SALOON OPEN sign to greet people to worship.

When they were seated inside, he stood in front of the sheet-draped bar and read Holy Scripture. He preached the Gospel in the dynamic way that only he could. And he led the congregation in prayer.

As a child, I considered this natural. My father was always concerned that people have a place to worship. I sang with them, played with them, visited in their homes with my father, and it never occurred to me that they were different from me.

Color of skin? Even as a child of the South in the forties, I truly did not notice!

One of the girls was named Marie. We became good friends and, with one of my other friends, formed a trio. We had a great sound. We sang night and day when we were together—whether people willingly listened or not!

To our delight, my father invited us to sing in our "white" church. When we stood up, even before we sang a note, I felt it. I didn't know what it was. But I knew it was something—and it crawled over my scalp with intensity. It continued even after we sat down.

After the service, a lady said to me coldly, "Don't you ever desecrate our church like that again."

And the light bulb came on.

She was "desecrated" because Marie was black.

How true is the poignant song of Rodgers and Hammerstein in the musical, *South Pacific:* "You've got to be taught to hate and fear . . ." to feel threatened by differences. If you don't know the words to this song, get a copy at your library and study them. It is an eloquent statement about prejudice.

"You've got to be carefully taught."

Although I had lived all ten of my years in the South, I had never had a moment's thought of prejudice. I had never once noticed the difference of a person's skin—*until I was told!*

Fortunately my parents were wiser teachers than the lady who admonished me after the service. Because of the furor caused that morning, my father asked us to sing that night.

"In spite of?" I asked, wide-eyed.

"In spite of," he told me firmly.

The next day I heard at school that some people were threatening to leave the church because of my father's work with black people. They had not cared until they had seen it before their eyes.

I went to my parents and told them I would explain to Marie; we would disband the trio. But they said no.

We would fight for what we believed right.

And we did.

Some of the people did leave the church. But my father continued his double ministry: in a white church and in a black saloon. In time, the black people built a beautiful church of their own where my father pastored until he left the city. And Marie, Jan, and I still had a great sound!

Prejudice can be "carefully taught." Prejudice can also creep in unaware.

When I was a student at The University of Kansas, I was subjected to a lengthy discourse in a speech class advocating segregation. I inwardly writhed in anger, sneering at the points that seemed so inane to me, hostile to the speaker in every fiber of my being.

He was a young man who had only recently joined one of our study groups and they were scheduled to come to my house before the next exam. I made mental note of the pleasure I would have in excluding him from the invitation list—when I suddenly paused and cringed in horror!

I was as guilty as he!

I was prejudiced against people who were prejudiced!

He wanted to exclude people from his circle of friends because of the color of their skin. I was determining to exclude him from my circle of friends because his ideas did not agree with my own.

I remembered a concept I had heard somewhere: love *includes;* prejudice *excludes.*

Regardless of the kind of prejudice, it is still narrowing and hampering. It rejects God's commandment to "love one another."

I was as guilty as my orating friend!

Prejudice is prejudice regardless of its form. It always excludes. It is always the opposite of God's love which includes.

Prejudice can invade many areas not normally considered.

When I was in junior high, there was an intense rivalry between our school and the junior high across town. We chanted cheers, jeers, and gossiped among ourselves as to how dreadful were the students of the other school.

I'll never forget when I attended the first game. I was shocked that those other kids looked so much like me and my friends. I had expected them to at least have horns, if not green skin with purple spots!

When I was a college professor a girl came to my office. She told me, in hushed tones, that she would like my help in appealing to the dean to get her another roommate. I asked her about the one she had, and she guardedly shared the shocking news that her roommate wore bikini pajamas; therefore she could not possibly be a Christian!

Ah! The prejudices that exclude people because of what they wear or do not wear! All that judgment—all that self-righteousness—all that exclusion—because of things!

I was in graduate school in the sixties. One of my colleagues was a typical hippie. He wore a long, shaggy, uncombed beard and hair and paint-spattered clothes; he had bare feet (even in the snow!) and lived in a commune at the edge of town. He wrote profane manuscripts of protest and read them with obvious delight in our class sessions.

I was a petite, minister's wife who wore bright colors, matching shoes, the latest hairdo, and lived with my husband and two children in a ten-room house with a fenced yard, swing set, and two Irish setters. I wrote romantic manuscripts of joy and read them with obvious delight in our class sessions.

Can't you already feel the sparks of prejudice flying?

I didn't understand hippies.

He didn't understand ministers' wives.

I couldn't imagine anyone living in a commune.

He couldn't imagine anyone living in a house with a husband, two kids, two dogs.

I had never heard his kind of language.

He had never heard my kind of language.

But oh! How we did learn!

I think, in many ways, he and I provided education to each other in more realms than did all of academia.

Graduate classes in creative writing are freewheeling. There is a constant give-and-take. It is interpersonally oriented between students rather than the professor–lecture format of undergraduate classes.

I remember one story I read which placed the parents of a beloved only son with the person responsible for his death. When I finished, my hippie was almost screaming, "That is the weirdest bunch of gibberish! Totally incredible! *Nobody* would ever act like that!"

He was pounding his desk in anger.

He leaned out to look at me. I returned his gaze in silence because I was so stunned.

The reactions of the parents in the story were identical to my own parents' reaction in a situation involving a similar tragedy. Just as he could not believe that anybody would act like that, I was astounded to consider that anybody would not act like that!

The rest of the class period was a dialogue between the two of us. The professor and students listened, and learned, as did we! The lesson had little to do with techniques of writing. It was concerned with how prejudice stems from experiential backgrounds.

Reared by agnostic parents, he thought of Christians as hypocritical frauds. My story portrayed Christians as genuinely strong, forgiving, including.

As we talked, he gained a view into my life experiences. And it began to break down his wall of prejudice against Christians. Whether or not he believed there was any validity to its theology, he became more open to including Christians in the realm of people he could respect.

Reared by religious parents, I thought that agnostics were ignorant rebels. In our discussion, he shared his life experiences in such dimension that my own wall of prejudice began to break down. These were people on the search—diligent, ongoing, sometimes desperate—people who had not yet found "answers to satisfy" their burning questions.

Although I had found a life-fulfilling center, I became open that day, as never before, to including people who have not chosen my theology, my life-style, my set of values. I became more open to including agnostics in the realm of people I could respect.

God's love always includes, reaches out to understand, strives to break down barriers of fear, yearns to shatter walls of the threatening unknown. "For God so loved the world that he gave his only begotten Son that whosoever believeth in him should not perish, but have everlasting life" (John 3:16).

When you open yourself for His love to flow through you, you will be better able to root out prejudices of all kinds whenever you find them cropping up: whether it is excluding someone because of the pajamas she wears . . . or because of her theological background!

God's love includes everyone. When you are open to Him, you will be open to all others with no room for prejudice.

Your love will always include.

How Can You Communicate With Your Parents?

2

I grew up in a happy home. I had wonderful parents who loved me; I loved them. We talked, laughed, played, prayed together.

Until I was fourteen.

At that point, our Garden of Eden turned into the raging wilderness. I screamed at my parents' rules. I strained at their boundaries. I deliberately verbally wounded them as only an articulate fourteen-year-old can.

I doubt that hell could be more unpleasant. We three were alienated from each other by impassable walls of fire.

They did not understand me. I did not understand them.

They were determined that I would live my life one way. I was determined I would fight them in every way I could devise.

When we weren't screaming, there was only a frozen, stiff, unbending silence. All of us were in agony.

One night Daddy was in his office as usual. Mother was on the sofa in the living room doing some mending. Because the light was best in that room, I pulled the sewing machine in there to work on a new dress I was making. But we didn't speak. There were only the sounds of the sewing machine in this room where I had known happiness.

After a while, my father came in.

I looked up in surprise. He always worked in his office until ten o'clock. Then he came home to listen to the news. It was his carefully kept schedule.

It was only about seven o'clock. I wondered what he was doing home.

I remember every moment of the following hour with vivid clarity. My father wearily sank into the big armchair next to the door. I noticed the lines in his face, the heavy sag of his body. And then he looked up at me with wistful longing.

My heart leaped with love for him, but I maintained my icy aloofness, dropped my eyes to my work, and began sewing a seam.

He didn't ask me to stop. With greater pain than I had ever heard in his voice before, he just began to talk. And, immediately, my sewing stopped and I listened.

Slowly, haltingly, from the depths of his heart, he began to tell me why he believed in the rules of our home, the boundaries he and Mother had set. He explained that the reasons lay in principles he had proven in his own life's mistakes.

My heart began jerking with such force I could not look at him. So I picked at a seam while his voice huskily detailed the errors he had made in his youth; the effect they had on his future life. He wanted to prevent my making those mistakes. For that reason, he had taken the stand from which he would not, could not, in love, move. He pleaded for me to understand.

My father cried.

This strong, wise man sat before his fourteen-year-old daughter and cried because he was in such pain over our losing each other.

And the iceberg that was my heart melted. Suddenly I jumped up from the sewing machine and by the time I got to him, he was standing with open arms. Mother joined us and we sobbed together, the three of us, and the room was close and warm—and very full.

From that point on, we could always talk.

He spent hours explaining himself to me so that I gained full understanding of why he made the decisions of parenting that he had. I didn't agree with him on all points. Not at all. But I understood. And that made the difference.

I agreed to live within the boundaries he set in our home. And I did. Even when they seemed silly to me, in my generation, I so deeply understood his reasoning and so respected his loving motive for the limits, that I lived within them. In peace. In the most tender love.

There comes a time in every home when parent and child face the problem of how to communicate across the barrier of generations. Sometimes it is never solved and pain remains in the hearts of all involved.

Few parents have the courage of my father. As I look back on that night, I believe he exhibited more sheer bravery in making himself vulnerable to his fourteen-year-old child than most men who wear war medals. It would be far easier to do some daring feat on a battlefield than to deliberately confront an angry teenager whom you loved with such depth that she could wound in a way that no bullet or torpedo ever could.

That night he did not know what my reaction would be. I could have continued to reject him. I could have cut, with hostile words, even deeper into his spirit. I could have left home. He knew all of that was possible. But he had enough strength of character and such a strong desire for unity with his child that he took the dare.

And he won.

We were heart-close through all of my teenage years. We were best friends through all of my adult life.

Solving the parent–child communication problem in this manner is rare. I was one of the lucky ones. I am profoundly grateful.

If you have a communication problem with your parents, and you feel fairly certain that it is not going to be solved as mine was, prayerfully consider how you might move to change it. Often, in my experience of counseling, when a girl has really opened herself to a strong relationship with her parents, they have responded beyond her expectations.

Not always. But when parents do not respond to an overture for peace and understanding from their child, it is usually because they cannot.

There are some people whose background or temperament is such that heart-sharing with a daughter (or with anyone) is an impossibility. When that is true for your parents, try to understand, accept, and love anyway. Remember, love includes, regardless of human limitations.

But because we cannot read other people's minds, we often accuse them of having attributes they do not.

So if this is a problem for you, prayerfully consider reaching out. Take the initiative, as did my father, to create unity and understanding. Just like me and my father, you may not find total agreement, but you may be able to work through the problems between you until you can live in peaceful harmony—and deep love.

When I lived in a parsonage one of my neighbors was a strong, silent woman. A marvelous cook, she gave joy to the entire block with her thoughtful gifts of hot rolls, brownies, and, in the summer, lemon ice cream.

She was always busy. She rarely said a word to anyone. She never chatted with me over the fence. She never made small talk when we met in the front yard.

She would listen, nod, smile. She would never talk.

As a result of her silence, her daughter, Cindy, who admired her inordinately, was afraid of her. She felt that her mother was perfection and she simply tried to live up to that.

In the tenth grade, Cindy met geometry and was in immediate confusion. I knew she was struggling, but I was not prepared for the storm of weeping that occurred in my den when she knew she had failed the subject for the term. I knew it was painful to fail, but I could not understand why she considered it so catastrophic. Finally, she told me of the perfection of her mother . . . how awful it was that she, her daughter, had failed.

I didn't know her mother's inner self either. I didn't know how she would react to failure. But I believe that most people yearn to share deeply, honestly, if there is an open door. So I urged Cindy to tell her mother how she felt. I urged her to earnestly try to share.

Still fearful, she asked if she could tell her on the phone.

I agreed.

She dialed the number and when she heard her mother's voice, she began to weep. She blurted out, "Mother, I failed geometry! Oh, Mother! I'm sorry I let you down! Mother, I'm sorry I failed!"

After a few moments, a look of incredulity came into Cindy's eyes. Then she said in a whisper, "I'll be right over."

She hung up the phone and we looked at each other, both wondering.

Then she gasped, "When I confessed that to Mother, she said, 'Come on home and let me tell you about all my failures. We'll find a way to handle this.' "

Cindy went home.

Later, she told me that she and her mother had talked for hours that afternoon. Finally, Cindy asked, "Why did you wait so long to share all of this with me?"

Her mother said, "I just never quite knew how. You have always been so bright, so competent. I didn't want to disappoint you!"

Cindy said, "Mother, I'm going to hug you. I've wanted to all my life and you've always been so busy that, for years, I haven't touched you. But I am going to hug you now. And every day and every night from now on."

And she did.

And does.

I asked Cindy if I could include the story in this book and she said, "Yes. Tell them that we are now a total embarrassment. In airports, we rush at each other with such fervor that we are gaped at on all sides."

I cannot promise that your parents will or can respond to you with a total sharing that would be ideal. But I can urge you to try.

And if it is an impossibility for them, try to understand why and love them anyhow! Focus on the fact that they care for you although it is not true to them (for whatever reason in their background) to give to you in the way you wish. Remember that they *do* love. That, after all, is the greatest gift they can give.

It is fashionable today to criticize parents, to blame parents, to disparage parents. Don't fall into that trap.

Your parents have done much for you. They have invested unselfishly in you. They would do, are doing, and have done their best for you. *Their best!*

Don't compare them to *The Brady Bunch* or *Father Knows Best* on television. Don't demand perfection. Don't even demand the level of communication your heart desires most. Strive to understand the who, the why of *your* parents. And when you can know them, in the context of all of their life-experiences, believe they have done and are doing their best for you. And be grateful.

With that gift, be willing to overlook the deficiencies, the fallibilities, the things that are less than ideal in the communication relationship. Instead, follow the admonition given in Philippians 4:8: "Whatsoever things are true, whatsoever things are honest, whatsoever things are just, whatsoever things are pure, whatsoever things are lovely, whatsoever things are of good report; if there be any virtue, and if there be any praise, think on these things."

How can you communicate with your parents?

Whoever they are . . . whoever you are . . . whatever are the possibilities of the degree of openness in communication, you can find the best possible for your unique family . . . in this mental focus. "Whatsoever" are the beauties, strengths, wonders in your home . . . think on these things.

God will help you move, in that mental sweetness, to the most open dimension of communication possible for the special people who form your important family circle.

How Can You Communicate With Others?

3

Open, honest sharing is vital in all interpersonal relationships. Communication with your parents is of special importance in your life. No matter how many brothers and sisters you may have, it is the ever-developing relationship between you and your parents that helps you learn how to communicate with every other person in your life.

One vital element is one's willingness to be vulnerable to another. My father had the raw courage to share with me deeply in order to establish a bond between us so that I could, in turn, share deeply with him.

I call it "raw courage" because the inner why's of another person are very precious, sacred, private. And when one shares them with another one runs the risk of the fragile inner-self being rejected or misunderstood. And when that happens, it is extremely painful because that essential core is our most basic gift.

I remember a young girl who sat in my office for what seemed hours. She needed help, but I could not get her to open up. She wrung the handkerchief in her hands; tears spilled down her cheeks occasionally; she made hesitant, awkward efforts at conversation, sometimes stabbing at the problem, but most of the time discussing my office decor or the latest chapel speaker.

I had been her academic counselor for the three years of her college life. She was bright, beautiful, charming, extraordinarily gifted in many ways.

Finally, she looked at me in total desperation and blurted out, "If I share this with you, I'll show you how stupid and weak I am in many areas and you may not like me!"

I understood what she was saying. It is the universal terror of exposing one's naked soul to another human being. Our brightness, beauty, and poise are so often facades. And we cower deep inside in the fear that someone might "find us out" for being "stupid and weak" in some areas of life and reject us.

It isn't that any of us, including my student, want to be fraudulent or play roles instead of being completely real. It is the fear of risking honesty so that one becomes vulnerable to another who "may not like" us anymore if we are not *always* bright, beautiful, and charming.

It is a dare, but it is an essential if there is to be open communication with another. In the last chapter, I gave the example of Cindy who had to take that dare with her mother before they could begin a heart-bond that has lasted through all of these years.

When my student in the counseling session blurted out, "If I share this with you ... you may not like me," I responded to her by assuring her that nothing she could say would change my loving admiration and respect for her. But I understood her fear because I had experienced it.

I told her some of the things I have written to you in this book—times when I have been both stupid and weak—so she could know I was not the all-wise professor I appeared in class. I, too, had human frailties and needed a friend to share with. I, too, felt terror in the sharing that the one hearing of my faults "might not like me anymore!"

When I took the first step into vulnerability, she was able to relax enough to trust me with her own frailties and needs. We had open communication because one of us took the dare of becoming vulnerable to the other.

Another imperative element in communication with others is the ability to "identify" with them ... or, to use an old cliché, "never judge a person until you have walked two miles in his moccasins." That was what my father let me do by allowing me to know the why's of his life, what it had been like for him in his childhood, early youth, early adulthood. Such identification, such personal understanding, will always improve any communication situation.

When I was seventeen, I had a radio show called "Piano Meditations" on our local station. In a nearby town, there was a small station whose manager told me that there was an elderly lady who had played on Sunday mornings for years. If she retired, they would be interested in having me perform there. I was excited at the thought of being on two stations, until I found out that the lady had refused to retire. Then I was angry. Angry until I asked myself, *How would I feel if the radio station manager wanted to take away my show?*

Devastated at the thought, I knew.

And yet it was only a small segment of my life's varied activities. I would be leaving it all, of my own volition, when I completed high school. No one would ever tell me I was too old for the piano show!

Everything was going my way. And yet I knew that, even now, it would hurt deeply if the station took such an action. How would I feel if it were the central core of my life—and had been for years?

I was so overwhelmed as I tried to identify with her that my anger melted into admiration for the lady's will power in continuing to play when it would have been easier to sit back and retire. I determined to meet her.

It was arranged.

She was gracious, charming, and spoke of her music with such affection I could hardly hold back the tears. I identified with her. When I did, all my personal resentment faded. More than that, I was glad that she had made the decision to continue her show. It meant more to her than it could possibly have meant to me.

"How would I feel if I were in that person's shoes?" is the key to identifying, which is one of the best doors in communicating with other people.

• When your little cousin has to have an appendectomy, if you can identify, you will be able to give meaningful support with your presence, a new teddy bear, and some hand-holding.
• When your best friend is entering an important contest, you can help her most if you can identify with her feelings of trepidation and give a constant stream of encouragement.
• When your teacher is abrupt with your class and you feel she's unfair, if you can identify with her frustration in trying to cover a certain amount of material in a limited time period, you will be more forgiving.

One of my students was deeply hurt by something her roommate had done. Her account made the roommate sound selfish, unfair, cruel.

But as we discussed identification, my student said, "I put myself in her place sometimes . . . and you know I can believe that she might have done this with my good in mind! She was wrong, but she could not have known that then!"

She thought about it for a while and then said, "But that scares me. Because when I identify with her, I can forgive her. And I don't know that she deserves forgiveness. I don't know that her motivation was my good."

"Can you know that it wasn't?" I queried.

She shook her head.

"In my experience with people, I have found most of them operate under good motives most of the time. When they don't, that still cannot change what I must do," I told her. "You know what that is?"

"Forgive," she said.

"Yes. Identifying and believing in pure motives will help in forgiveness. Even when you know it was a selfish, even cruel, motive, identifying to see why such an act was necessary to that person will help you forgive."

In an earlier chapter, I quoted from a letter my mother wrote to me. In it was a poem that formed the credo of her life. I chose it as the credo of my own life. It works every time.

> When I am terribly upset with another person, I whisper:
> If I could only see the road you came
> The jagged rocks and crooked ways,
> I would more kindly think of your mis-step
> And only praise.
>
> If I could know the heartaches you have felt,
> The longings for the things that never came,
> I would not harshly judge your erring then
> Nor even blame.

Another important element in communicating with others is to understand communication that is not put into words. It is harder and demands your truly focusing on the other person, wanting to understand. But it is a truly effective channel for sharing.

I first noticed it as a teenager when I went to the home of one of my friends for a weekend. On Saturday afternoon, we were sitting on the swing on her porch with nothing to do. Her father, a silent man who had spoken only a few times during my visit and then in harsh, loud tones, came out. He leaned against the porch railing for a few minutes and then, abruptly, wheeled to his daughter, angrily thrust some bills into her hands and said in a rough voice, "I hear the carnival's in town; take this and you two get out of my way!"

I was horrified. I felt myself cringing from the man who seemed so hostile to us. My friend jumped up, kissed him soundly, and said, "Thanks, Dad!" We were off for a fun-filled afternoon at the carnival.

She had sensed my response to the scene. When we were far enough away from the house so we could not be heard, she looked at me with sparkling eyes, happy smile, and said, "You didn't know it, but my father just said, 'I love you and I want you and your friend to be happy.' "

I stared at her incredulously.

And then she explained that her father had been born illegitimately; he never knew his father; his mother hated him because of the stigma his birth brought to her personally; his grandparents, with whom he and his mother lived, thought him a "disgrace to the family." In such an environment, he had grown up.

His response, of course, was to withdraw within himself. And when he had to speak, he came out with the same verbal anger that had been hurled at him. He knew nothing of love or softness or giving tenderness until he had met her mother.

Her mother understood him; they had a beautiful, although chiefly silent, marriage. And her mother had enabled her, their child, to understand, to *identify* with her father. She had become so skillful in receiving nonverbal communication that the two had a strong, incredibly wonderful love-bond between them.

It was a life-changing lesson to me. I had heard a tough, loud voice saying angry words, "Get out of my way!" My friend identified with her father. She understood the words he chose. She had "heard" the truth. "I love you," her father said in the only way he knew how, "and I want you and your friend to be happy."

Later, when I was a minister's wife, I had an active program for our teens. Our janitor was an elderly man with loud voice and angry words. At first I was afraid of him. But as I got to know him better, we became best friends. That was possible because I learned to communicate with him as my friend had with her father.

One night, there was a party in the recreation room with an unusual quantity of decorations. As the activity was concluding, he came in to survey what his cleanup job would be. He said to me in a gruff voice, "You keep this room messed up more than all the rest of the church put together! I've had to work harder since you came here than when I worked on board ship!" (He had been a professional fisherman in his early life.)

The words stung until I looked at him. His eyes were glowing with affection; there was a warmth in them that reached out to me with such force I could almost touch it. I remembered my friend's lesson and I understood that he had just said, "You're doing a grand job keeping these kids busy." And, as I studied his face, I believed that in those rough complaining words, he also had said, "I love you."

On impulse, I kissed his white-bearded chin. He grinned and pushed me away. Then I knew I had been right. We had just exchanged honest communication. From then on, no matter how he said it or what words he used, I knew he was my strongest supporter and my caring friend.

Words are not the *only* way of communicating with others. Words are not the *only* way of receiving important messages. Be sensitive to the people in your world who cannot talk freely and openly. Be willing to go beyond words, when necessary, to find a way of giving and receiving with another on whatever level is comfortable to that person.

One other important principle in communicating with others is this: accept others without judgment. This is difficult, but if you will develop it in all of life, others will observe it, come to trust it, and be more willing to open themselves to you honestly.

Recently, I received a letter from a friend. She wrote, "You can know that whatever you say, whatever you do, I will never judge you. I believe in you so much that even if I am surprised at something, I will know there is a good reason for it. I will never, ever judge you. You can rely on that."

Consciously decide to believe in others as you attempt to communicate with them. It begins by proving yourself unjudgmental in all of your conversations. It develops strong sharing with others as they dare to be vulnerable to you and find you never judging harshly, but always reaching for accepting understanding.

Make your life creed—and prove it in your conversation every day—*love always includes.* Love is not judgmental. Love accepts under all circumstances. Love never fails.

When you give that gift to other people in your life, you will be able to communicate with them—and they with you. And your life will glow with the radiance of God's kind of love.

How Can You
Be of Service to Others?

4

There you are!

We have discussed, in several places in this book, that there are two kinds of people in the world: *Here I am!* and *There you are!* I believe that the most succinct and complete answer to the question "How can you be of service to others?" lies in your willingness to focus on other people. The answer lies simply in approaching others and saying, "There you are!"

I remember when I was a young minister's wife, I went to a retreat. The speaker took my breath away. She was witty, warm, wonderful! I hung on her every word and tried to memorize her every phrase.

Later, in an informal sharing time, she came to sit beside me. Breathlessly, I told her how terrific she was and how much she had helped me by sharing her wisdom. She listened for only a few moments to all of this and then she said, looking me straight in the eyes, "Thank you very much. I'm glad you like me. Now tell me about you. What have you been doing with your life? Where are you now? What are your goals?"

I was thunderstruck that she wanted to spend her valuable time listening to me. But it was the most beautiful gift, the most loving service she could have given me. She made me, a very young, inexperienced girl, seem of great value. She pointedly decided that the brief time we would have for informal conversation should be centered upon me!

I have never forgotten the moment.

And it is a quality I have earnestly tried to develop. She was the "star" of the occasion, and I would have listened to her every word with deepest appreciation for her honoring me with her wisdom. But she rendered me greater service by being willing to listen to me and make me feel important in my life and in my dreams.

There you are!

It is easy for us to chatter about ourselves. It is much more difficult to truly *listen* with all of one's being to another—sharing tears, laughter, fears, joy—hand-holding in life.

My "adopted niece" married recently. I wrote her a long letter in which I advised her to listen to her mate intently, trying to understand all the things he was saying, all the things he was feeling but might not be saying.

When she wrote back, she said, "I had never thought of that in regard to listening. I've always listened only long enough to think of a retort and get the conversation back to me!"

I think that is true of most of us most of the time unless we deliberately train ourselves to be different. *Here I am!* is such a fun, happy, easy place to be; it takes strength of character to genuinely turn the spotlight to another and listen with deep intensity, truly wanting to understand.

How can you be of service to others?

There you are!

One means of developing that answer is listening, really listening, to someone else. Another is *believing* in the potential of another.

Fannie Crosby, a blind poet, wrote a marvelous poem which was set to music. It is the old hymn, "Rescue the Perishing." Here is one stanza:

> Down in the human heart,
> Crushed by the tempter,
> Feelings lie buried
> That grace can restore:
> Touched by a loving heart,
> Wakened by kindness,
> Chords that were broken
> Will vibrate once more.

And the chorus goes: Rescue the perishing, care for the dying;
Jesus is merciful, Jesus will save.

I know some literary "experts" who mark this off as too sentimental. But whatever its technical attributes, I find its content vital.

There you are! Fannie Crosby's poem is a wonderful way to approach being of service to others. No matter how broken a life may be, no matter how great are the mistakes that have been made, no matter how much sin a human being has experienced, God is Redeemer of circumstance as well as of sin. There is hope for fulfilling life for everyone who desires it, walks with God, and has a human being to believe in him.

My mother believed the best of everyone in every circumstance. It was incredible, even to her children who knew her best, but she was able to achieve some astonishing results with the broken lives that came to our parsonage door.

One of them was a young man who had been orphaned early in life. He had been thrown "from pillar to post," as my mother phrased it, in his growing years. She meant that one uncaring relative had passed him to another and on down the line until he was old enough to take on his own independence.

He did so with gusto. He was a constant saloon brawler, in and out of jail almost monthly. He finally ended up in such serious trouble that he was going to be sent to prison. My parents went to court for him because he frequently attended our church. They asked that he be released in their custody.

I remember their bringing him home for supper that night. He was dirty, ill-kempt, unshaven, had bad breath and a pervading body odor, and ate with his hands! I had never seen anyone in such a state and could only look on in silent horror.

My parents conversed with him as if he were our most honored guest. And I noticed, even then, that the conversation centered on all that he could become.

I listened with stark skepticism. But I kept my own counsel. I never discussed it with my parents.

As the months went by, I saw the transformation.

Not only did he appear in clothes my mother had obtained from people of the church who had sons his size, but he kept them clean. For my mother. I also noted he kept himself shaven and clean-smelling. I was certain that was also for my mother.

He kept the job my father had gotten him in a grocery and he came to our house twice a week where my mother gave him all her "school-teaching" skills. It seemed a short time until we had a party celebrating his graduation from high school (done by correspondence).

That fall he went to college. He graduated four years later. He went to the seminary. Today he is a successful pastor.

He tells me every time he sees me that this incredible story is true for one reason only: My mother believed in him. I didn't know then that there were times he gave it all up and went out and got drunk; I didn't know then that there were times he would hurl his books across the room because he could not understand the concepts my mother was trying to teach; I did not know then that, once, he even cursed her for trying to make him "into something [he] wasn't!"

But he tells me these things now. He tells me that she accepted it all calmly, as a matter-of-course; and when he was finished with his tantrums, she would simply take up where they had left off—always believing in him.

When he tells me, I can see my mother's face. I can hear her voice as she used to quote to me Fannie Crosby's words, "Down in the human heart crushed by the tempter, feelings lie buried that grace can restore. . . ."

She believed that so much that she made it come true. In more lives than I could recount in an entire volume. She was a *There you are!* person: not only in her willingness to focus on the other person; not only in her willingness to listen carefully to the other person; but also by believing in the finest potential of the other person.

This is a gift that is not reserved for the mature to give the younger as evidenced in the example of my mother. It may also be given to your peers.

One of my college friends was an excellent writer. But she was terribly shy. A young man who worked on the local newspaper observed her ability in a writing class. He took her out for coffee, urging her to believe in her potential. She finally agreed to talk to his editor. She got the job and is a reporter on a large city newspaper today. It never would have happened, she would be quick to tell you, if a peer, a friend her own age, had not given her the gift of believing in her talent and urging her to develop it.

It can also be a gift from the young to older people. When one of my high school chums graduated, she suggested that her mother, who had never gone to college, enroll with her as a freshman. At first, her mother chided the idea. But with our urging her to believe in what she could do, she did enroll. Four years later, she graduated with straight A's, a degree in music, and a career in teaching music ahead of her.

How can you be of service to others? Believe in their finest potential. Encourage them to believe in themselves and reach to make their dreams come true.

People who truly care about and focus on others create an atmosphere of joy, cheer, and happiness about themselves. Robert Louis Stevenson wrote, "There is no duty we so much underrate as the duty of being happy."

My students used to be startled when we studied this piece of Stevenson's writing. They had never considered being happy a duty. But I believe it is, and I surely believe it is imperative if you truly want to be of service to others, if you want to be a *There you are!* kind of person.

My students often argued that happiness was not something that could be controlled. "You're either happy or not happy," one of them wrote me one time. "You just have to take what comes and if it's unhappy, then you're unhappy. You're wrong when you say it is something that can be developed, like a duty!"

Many people believe they are the victims of external events. Many people believe they are happy or unhappy depending on "what comes," as my student wrote. But they are wrong. Our emotions are determined by our own choices.

The best key to this is given in Philippians 4:6 which I quoted earlier: "Whatsoever things are true, whatsoever things are honest, whatsoever things are just, whatsoever things are pure, whatsoever things are lovely, whatsoever things are of good report; if there be any virtue, and if there be any praise, think on these things."

You choose the thoughts you think. You choose the elements of life on which you focus.

What shall be the atmosphere of your life?

Drab or glowing . . . light or bright . . . frowns or smiles . . . You choose! And, in that choice, not only lies your own happiness, but also the happiness of those about you. In that choice is a vital element in being of service to others.

The best example I have seen of this was my mother.

Confined to a wheelchair for years, her debilitating illness finally felled her to her bed. Ultimately, it claimed her eyesight.

I remember asking her one day why she was so eternally cheerful! "Don't you *mind?*" I asked, almost in exasperation.

She smiled. "Of course, I mind, but I keep my mental focus on the 'good report' of the unfailing, amazing, everlasting love of my husband, the achievements of my three tall sons, the happiness that my little girl gives me every day . . . and when cushioned by gratitude, the unpleasant things fade into the background."

My mother chose to be a *There you are!* person even in a rest home, even when confined to bed, even when stricken blind. She was of service to every person around her because she chose to make the atmosphere about her so cheerful.

She could have been yelling, complaining, self-pitying. She could have whined, whimpered, or withdrawn. She could have (justifiably in those circumstances) been a *Here I am!* person and demanded more than others could possibly give.

Instead she made a deliberate choice that the atmosphere about her would be one of "sunshine." When she was alone, she told me that she kept her mind busy by quoting poetry to herself, reciting familiar pieces backwards, and playing number games she made up in her head. When others were about, she would dismiss queries about her health with, "I hope I'm better," which was always true whether, in fact, she was better or not. Then she would ask, "But what about you? Tell me about your life."

She was loved by doctors, nurses, and every person who touched her life in that rest home. Why? Because she made the deliberate choice to be of service to others; by being a *There you are!* person; by creating a joyful, sunshiny, happy atmosphere about her so that others came to bask in it.

How can you be of service to others?

Philippians 4:6 spells it out for you. It may be succinctly summarized in the phrase we have used in this book: *There you are!*

How Can You Be a Beautiful Woman in Your World?

5

It may be best to begin exploring the answer to that question by looking at where you are now.

What is it *to be a girl?*

It is to be a mixture of contradictions . . . you are no longer a child . . . you are not yet a woman . . .

Your identity is still forming . . .

You are still searching to discover the full reality of *who you are* . . . and so everything about your life is in flux.

Nothing is the same for you.

Not your body.

Not your emotions.

Not other people's expectations of you.

Not other people's responses to you.

Not your future . . .

Everything is changing . . . and change is always frightening.

Change spotlights things disproportionately:

When you are feeling low, you hit the deepest bottom of the ocean-bed

157

... while your up-moments are in the glory of moon-orbit.

Your disappointments destroy you like a collapsed tinker toy ... in a million pieces ... hopelessly beyond repair ... while your laughter on dates, at parties, on the telephone goes on and on and on and on and on and ...

Your fears are ten feet tall with four heads and twelve forked tongues ... while your excitement is served in forty-foot mugs large enough to swim in.

Change whirls you, like a clock pendulum, from one extreme emotion to another:

You are reaching for the future.
You are pulling back into the security of the past.

You are straining for independence.
You are snuggling in the comfort of dependence.

You are yearning to be a competent, mature, on-your-own-feet "I."
You are resting in the safety of being a part of "we": daughter, sister, student, friend.

Change.
That is what it is to be a girl.
That is why you feel all the contradictions right now.
That assures you that you're a bright, growing, *normal* girl.

What is it to be a girl?
What is it ... to turn that corner right there beside you ...
                    the corner you want to turn so badly and yet ...
                        you are terrified to walk around ...
What is it ... to turn   t
                         h
                         a
                         t corner and to be a woman?

It can be stated simply.
To be a girl is to know the joy of receiving.
To be a woman is to turn the corner and claim the joy of creative giving.
It's that simple.
It's that difficult.
Because you know, deep inside, that once you turn that corner, nothing will ever be the same for you again.

For this is fact: To be a woman is to be a creator
a nourisher
a giver.

This is fact: God created the feminine heart so that its strongest instinct is to bear responsibility in creating newness, in nourishing growth.

When you turn that corner, you will hear a hundred voices calling you to follow them in a hundred directions. A girl will be confused, caught off balance, bewildered as to whom to follow. A woman will have set her eyes on Jesus with such straightforward gaze that she gives no heed to other voices calling to other paths. She will, as maturely as she can, follow in His steps.

In that confidence, a woman can turn the girlhood corner with certainty, poise, assurance. And when you do, you will be accepting accountability for your own actions and decisions. You will be working toward the mature charting of your life, toward your personal dreams-come-true. You will be claiming confidence in your abilities to do a job on your own.

And you can do it.

Don't be ashamed of the fears, the butterfly-stomp in the stomach at the challenge of change. That is normal. Jesus understands all about it and He will take your terror-dampened palm into His own and
turn   t
h
a
t corner with you. He will help you change from receiver to giver. And that is what it means to change a girl into a woman.

And to be a woman is to experience life's supreme adventure.

To help you better understand that last statement, let me share with you a letter my husband wrote me. He is usually one of the world's most unpoetic people. But, occasionally, he surprises me.

A few months ago, he was attending a seminar where one of the lecturers was an extremist in the women's liberation movement. That night, he sat in his hotel and penned me a letter I shall always cherish. Share part of it with me:

> I have heard for the last several hours the thesis that women are no different from men. I sit here, look at your picture, and thank God that is not true.
>
> I ponder on the gifts you give to me *because you are uniquely woman.* These are some of the things that quickly come to mind.
>
> You are my love. Not only is your body uniquely my love, but the soft, tender, giving spirit that prompts your caresses and kisses is my love.

In that feminine charm, you delight me in every quest for love.

"You turn the world on with your smile." I know that's like a line from Mary Tyler Moore's theme song, but it is one I often hum when I think of you. Your warm smile in that small womanly face is the focus for making my whole world . . . not only go round . . . but make sense. It is a woman's gentle, understanding, joyful smile that "turns on my world." I live with the texture of men; what I need most from you is the special glow of femininity.

"You Light Up My Life!" is Debby Boone's song. But, again, it runs through my head day after day as I thank God for you. We have faced life in all of its moods. In the sunshine, you have outshone the orange ball. Your excited joy spilled all over me and, although I can't jump and shout and rhapsodize as you can, its expression makes my happiness more complete. In the midnight of life, you have been a radiant glow that always gave me "hope to carry on."

No. Anyone who advocates that the difference between man and woman is totally physical is unthinking . . . or has never known a real woman. I would say: The soul of a woman is the candle of God. Men grow in its glow.

Can there be greater beauty you can give to your world?

To be a woman is to be an unfaltering flame to "light up the world." To be a woman is to possess such a radiant, illuminating, enhancing sparkle that "men grow in its glow." To be a woman is to be "the candle of God!"

> Lovingly open to all you know
> With your flaming inner candle-glow
> And your soul
> Whole
> Daring to be the candle of God
> To all lives you touch
> On earthen sod . . .
> You are becoming a woman!

It is the most wonderful feeling in the world!
  Rejoice in it.
  And give thanks.